Improve your Skills

Listening & Speaking for IELTS

with Answer Key

6.0–7.5

Joanna Preshous

MACMILLAN

Macmillan Education
4 Crinan Street
London N1 9XW
A division of Macmillan Publishers Limited

Companies and representatives throughout the world

ISBN 978-0-230-46341-7 (with key + Audio Pack)
ISBN 978-0-230-46343-1 (without key + Audio Pack)
ISBN 978-0-230-46342-4 (with key + Audio + MPO Pack)
ISBN 978-0-230-46763-7 (without key + Audio + MPO Pack)

Designed by Kamae Design, Oxford
Illustrated by Kamae Design, p16, 17, 21, 32, 33, 37, 77.
Cover design by Macmillan
Cover photograph by Getty Images/Remi Mansi
Picture research by Susannah Jayes

Author's acknowledgements
The author would like to thank Andrew, Laura and Eleanor for their support and
encouragement throughout this project.
Special thanks to the freelance editor for her valuable advice and guidance.
The author would like to dedicate this book to her parents.

The publishers would like to thank all those who participated in the development of the
project, with special thanks to the freelance editor.

The author and publishers would like to thank the following for permission to reproduce
their photographs:
Alamy/Ange p38(bl), Alamy/Carmo Correia p54, Alamy/Greatstock Photographic Library
p38(cl); **Bananastock** p26; **Brand X** p20; **Corbis** p64, Corbis/Hero Images p30, Corbis/
Imaginechina p14(bl), Corbis/Helen King p14(cl), Corbis/Edvard March p62(bl), Corbis/
Ariel Skelley p62(bcl), Corbis/William Whitehurst p70; **Creatas** p78(tl);
Getty Images p25, Getty Images/Anne Ackermann p38(bcl), Getty Images/Heungman
Kwan p46(cl), Getty Images/Lisa Mckelvie p6(c), Getty Images/Cohen/Ostrow p6(a);
Glow Images/Adam Haglund p6(b); **Image Source** p78(tm); **Macmillan Publishers
Ltd** p57; **PIXTAL** p78(tr); **Thinkstock**/Getty Images p46(cr), Thinkstock/Istockphoto
pp62(cl),78(cr).

Although we have tried to trace and contact copyright holders before publication, in
some cases this has not been possible. If contacted we will be pleased to rectify any
errors or omissions at the earliest opportunity.

Printed and bound in Thailand

2018 2017 2016 2015 2014
10 9 8 7 6 5 4 3 2 1

Contents

Introduction

What is *Improve your IELTS Listening and Speaking Skills?*

Improve your *IELTS Listening and Speaking Skills* is a complete preparation course for students at score bands 6.00-7.5 preparing for the for the Listening and Speaking components of the International English Language Testing System. Through targeted practice, it develops skills and language to help you achieve a higher IELTS score in these two components.

How can I use this book?

You can use *Improve your IELTS Listening and Speaking Skills* as a book for studying on your own or in a class.

If you are studying on your own, *Improve Your IELTS Listening and Speaking Skills* is designed to guide you step by step through the activities. The book is completely self-contained: a clear and accessible key is provided, so you can easily check your answers as you work through the book. There are two CDs which contain all the recorded material necessary for the Listening skills and Speaking skills sections of each unit.

If you are studying as part of a class, your teacher will direct you on how to use each activity. Some activities, especially in the Topic talk and Speaking skills sections, provide the opportunity for speaking and discussion practice.

How is *Improve your IELTS Listening and Speaking Skills* organized?

It consists of ten units based around topics which occur commonly in the real test. Each unit consists of:

Topic talk: exercises and activities to introduce vocabulary and ideas useful for the topic.

Listening skills: exercises and activities to develop the skills for questions in the Listening component.

Speaking skills: exercises and activities to develop skills and language for the Speaking component, including practice questions from one part of the module.

Pronunciation: exercises and activities to practise key aspects of pronunciation in English.

Exam listening: one complete section of the Listening exam to practise the skills learned.

In addition, there are *Techniques* boxes throughout the book. These reinforce key points on how to approach Listening and Speaking tasks.

How will *Improve your IELTS Listening and Speaking Skills* improve my score?

By developing skills

The skills sections of each unit form a detailed syllabus of essential IELTS Listening and Speaking skills. For example, in Listening skills there is coverage of *Predicting in notes* and *Labelling a map or plan*. In Speaking skills, there is coverage of *Giving extended answers* as well as *Agreeing and disagreeing*. There is also a Pronunciation section at the end of the Speaking skills sections.

By developing language

The *Topic talk* part of each unit develops vocabulary, phrases, and sentence forms for use in the Listening and Speaking components. The Speaking skills section has phrases to help you introduce and organize your spoken answers.

By developing test technique

The Listening skills sections introduce you to the skills you need to tackle the various types of question that can be asked. Knowing the best way to tackle each type of question will enable you to get the best mark you can. The Speaking skills section will make you familiar with the different question-types and enable you to relax in the exam and perform at your best.

How is the IELTS Listening component organized?

It consists of four sections: usually there are two monologues and two conversations on a variety of topics. There are ten questions in each section. The topics cover everyday social matters and subjects related to educational or training situations. You hear the recording only once, but you have time to look at the questions first and further time to write your answers. The exam lasts approximately 40 minutes (which includes 10 minutes to transfer your answers).

What kind of questions are there?

There are a variety of question types including multiple choice, matching, short answer questions, sentence completion, form/table completion, labelling a diagram/plan/map, classification of information, matching information, and summary.

How will I be assessed?

You will get one mark for each correct answer up to a maximum of 40 marks. The questions get gradually harder, but all the marks have the same value.

How is the IELTS Speaking component organized?

You have a one-to-one interview with an examiner lasting between eleven and fourteen minutes. There are three parts. First, the examiner asks questions on everyday topics such as family, hobbies, and likes and dislikes. Second, you speak for one to two minutes on a topic given by the examiner. Finally, you take part in a discussion on more abstract issues linked to the topic of the talk.

How will I be assessed?

The examiner awards marks under four headings:

Fluency and coherence: speaking in a continuous way, without unnatural hesitation, and organizing your thoughts and speech in a logical way.

Lexical resource: using a range of vocabulary appropriate to the topic.

Grammatical range and accuracy: using a range of grammatical forms, including more complex forms, with a reasonable degree of accuracy.

Pronunciation: speaking so that you can be understood by the examiner.

LISTENING SKILLS
Identifying the context
Predicting in notes

SPEAKING SKILLS
Part 1: Talking about familiar topics
Giving extended answers

PRONUNCIATION
Word linking 1

EXAM LISTENING
Section 1

starting school a

get married b

celebrating significant birthday c

Topic talk

1 Look at the pictures and answer the questions below.

  a Which life events do the photographs show?

  b What other major events in a person's life can you think of? Which ones have you already experienced?

  c Which milestones are particularly important in your culture?

2 Match the words and phrases in the box with the descriptions (a–h) below.

> a place of your own ■ career ■ degree ■ driving test ■ early retirement ■ family
> gap year ■ sabbatical ■ voluntary work

Example
I've worked for fifteen years in the same industry and although I've been successful, I feel it's time to move on to something different. ___career___

  a I spend two afternoons a week at a local charity; I visit elderly people in my neighbourhood and do odd jobs for them. _voluntary work_

  b I'm very nervous as I've already failed twice; I really want to get a licence so that I can be more independent. _driving test_

  c We had our first child last year so at the moment I'm a stay-at-home mum – it's hard work! _family_

  d My work has given me a year off so that I can write my book; I'm also planning to travel to Australia. I'm so excited! _sabbatical_

  e I intend to stop working by the time I'm 55; I've been working since I was 15 so I think I'm due some relaxation. _early retirement_

  f When I leave school I'm not going straight to university; I'd like to work for a few months to save some money and then go travelling. _____

  g After three years' hard work I'm finally going to graduate; my whole family is coming to the ceremony. _gap year_

  h I'd like to be independent and move away from home; I'd miss my mum's cooking though! _a place of your own_

Technique

Using the correct collocation will make you sound more accurate in your speaking and will gain you marks in the IELTS Speaking test.

3 Match the phrases in the box in 2 with the verbs below to form collocations. Then rewrite the sentences using the collocations. Some of the verbs may be used more than once.

| change ▪do ▪get ▪pass ▪start ▪take |

[handwritten notes:]
change career
do voluntary job
get degree / place of your own
take sabbatical / early retirement / gap year
pass driving test

Example
I've worked for fifteen years in the same job for the same company and now I feel it's time to __change career__ .

4 Which of the life experiences in 3 have you already had? Which do you intend to do in the future? When do you hope to do them? Which do you think you will never do? Why?

5 The adjectives (a–g) below can all be used to describe life events and experiences. In each case decide which one is the opposite of the other two.
  a disappointing/rewarding/fulfilling
  b unremarkable/unforgettable/memorable
  c challenging/tough/straightforward
  d once in a lifetime/ordinary/special
  e trying/frustrating/satisfying
  f dull/stimulating/exciting
  g life-changing/insignificant/momentous

6 Which of the adjectives in 5 have positive meanings? Which are negative? Which are neither positive nor negative?

7 Which adjectives could you use to describe the events and experiences in 2? How would you describe some of your own life experiences?

8 Complete each of the statements below with an example from your own life.
  a A challenging experience I remember was …
  b A disappointing experience I had was …
  c A memorable journey I took was …
  d A life-changing decision I made was …
  e An exciting holiday I had was …
  f A frustrating experience I had was …

9 Choose one of the experiences in 8 and talk to your partner about it. Try to develop your ideas with reasons and examples.

Exam information

In Speaking Part 2 you may be asked to talk about an experience or event in your life. Use adjectives to describe the event and how it made you feel.

Unit 1

Listening skills

Identifying the context

1 Choose the correct context (1–4) for each set of notes (A–D).

1 a telephone message
2 a language school enrolment form
3 notes about a product
4 lecture notes

Exam information

You may have to complete notes in any section of the Listening test. In the exam you will hear a short introduction to each section on the recording and then you will have some time to read the notes

A → 3

Model: **1** ....

Colours available: black, **2** ....

Total charge (including delivery): **3** ....

B → 2

Name: Yue Chen

Test score: **4** ....

Tutor: **5** ....

Classroom: 12

C → 4

Common name: Grey Seal

Habitat: open sea, **6** ...., sandy beaches.

Weight: males (bulls): **7** ....; females (cows): 100–200 kg

Breeding season: September to **8** ....

D → 1

Name of caller: James Fisher

Contact number:

9 ....

Call back: before

10 ....

Predicting in notes

2 Match the different types of information below (a–j) with the information required in the gaps (1–10) in 1.

  a a price
  b a measurement
  c a reference number
  d a number
  e a month
  f a name
  g a colour
  h a time
  i a place
  j a telephone number

Technique

Try to quickly identify the situation from the notes and from the introduction on the recording. You should then spend the time before the dialogue starts thinking about the situation and predicting the type of language you might hear.

3 🔊 1.1–1.4 Listen and complete the notes in 1 with NO MORE THAN TWO WORDS AND/OR A NUMBER for each answer.

4 Now match the extra information (a–h) below with the correct set of notes in 1.

  a Offer available until: _____

  b Hunted for: _____ , blubber, _____

  c Message: interested in _____ for sale

  d Number of offspring: _____

  e Message for: _____

  f Weekly fee: _____

  g Extra features: _____ , guarantee

  h Hours per week: _____

  i Diet: variety of _____

  j Level: _____

5 Complete the gaps (a–j) in 4 with the information below. Then listen again to check your answers.

> 16 ■ £132 ■ bike ■ free case ■ fish ■ Helen Black
> intermediate ■ one ■ skin, meat ■ Sunday

Unit 1

Speaking skills

Part 1: Talking about familiar topics

Exam information

In Part 1 of the Speaking test the examiner will ask you questions on familiar topics such as your home town, your family, your studies and interests.

1 🔊 1.5–1.10 Listen to six candidates answering questions from Part 1 of the Speaking test. What question do you think the examiner asked in each case? Complete the examiner's questions.

a How _____ ?

b What _____ ?

c Do _____ ?

d Do _____ ?

e How _____ ?

f Do _____ ?

Technique

Listen carefully to how the examiner starts the question. This will help you decide what type of answer you should give, e.g. if a question starts with *Why ...?*, you will be expected to give a reason.

2 The candidates in 1 use linking expressions (e.g. *and, so, because*) to link ideas and sentences together and help them give extended answers. Complete Candidate 1's answer below with linking expressions, then listen again to check your answers.

I came by bus. **1** .... I had to take two different buses **2** ....
my home is on the other side of the city and the whole journey took about 45 minutes. I like travelling by bus **3** .... I don't do it very often **4** .... I usually walk or cycle to school, **5** .... is really near my home. I only use it if I want to go on a longer journey **6** .... into the city centre. Today I had quite a long distance to travel and **7** .... I came by bus.

3 Which items in 2 have the following functions?

a to give a reason _____

b to give an example _____

c to add extra information _____

d to give a consequence _____

e to show contrast _____

Technique

Always try to give extended answers by giving reasons, examples and any other extra information that is relevant. Do not memorize long speeches as this will sound unnatural and will lose you marks.

4 Look at the audio script and find other examples of linking words.
Add the examples to the list in 3.

5 With a partner, ask and answer the questions in 1.
Make sure you give extended answers.

Giving extended answers

6 Write 10 questions using the prompts, one for each of the topics below.
Examples
Who do you live with? (accommodation)
How often do you eat in a restaurant? (food)

> accommodation ■ daily routines ■ entertainment ■ family
> food ■ holidays ■ interests ■ shopping ■ studies ■ work

a Who _____ ?

b How long _____ ?

c Do _____ ?

d Have _____ ?

e When _____ ?

f What _____ ?

g How often _____ ?

h Which _____ ?

i Why _____ ?

j Would _____ ?

7 Look at the possible questions in 6. Match the extended answers below to four of the questions.
Then mark the linking words.

1 I like going to the cinema if it's a new film or a film that has special effects because it's much better to see it on a large screen and going with friends means we can talk about it afterwards. I live in a small village 30 km from the nearest cinema though, so going to the cinema is quite expensive. I also have to go in the early evening as the last bus to my village leaves the town at 10.30 pm. And watching at home is much cheaper than going to the cinema! _____

2 I'm a student so most of my time is spent at lectures and in the library. But I have a job in a local café near the university to help pay for things. I work three evenings a week serving customers and I also help out in the kitchen. I can eat there on the evenings I work, which also helps with my finances! I sometimes work on Saturday too, but I like to keep the weekend free if I can. _____

3 I play badminton and I'm a member of my college team – we play against other college teams and we're quite good. As a spectator I enjoy going to see my local football team and watching bigger matches on television. I like watching tennis tournaments too – it's really interesting to see players who play very well on one surface but not necessarily on another. _____

4 I like going shopping with my sister. There's a big shopping centre in the town where we live and we often go there at the weekend to look around the shops and have coffee. There's an ice rink there too, so we sometimes take my little brother, but he doesn't like shopping! If I need to buy something expensive like new shoes then I'll go with my mum, because she can pay for them! _____

8 With a partner, ask and answer the questions you made in 6.
Give extended answers using the words and phrases from 4.

Unit 1

Pronunciation: word linking

1 When a word begins with a vowel sound and the previous word ends in a consonant sound, we link the two sounds together in continuous natural speech. Listen again to candidate 2 on page 10 speaking and note how he links his words.

> What I like most is the fact that it's near the coast because I love the sea. I always try to go there at weekends. I also think it has good facilities – there's plenty to do, particularly for young people as there's a leisure centre and swimming pool, two cinemas and a large shopping centre. One thing I don't like is that we don't have many parks or green spaces so there aren't many nice places to walk or play.

2 Mark the linking in these statements.

   a I'd like to get a place of my own as soon as I can.

   b I hope I can take early retirement before I'm sixty.

   c I'd like to start a family when I'm about thirty years old.

   d Next year I'm planning to take a sabbatical so that I can travel to South America.

   e I've always wanted to get a degree in electronic engineering.

   f I can't afford to take a gap year unless I can get a job and save up.

Technique

Linking your words together will make you sound more natural and fluent. Remember it is the sounds that link, not the letters, e.g. *like is* links together because the final sound of /laɪk/ links with the initial sound of /ɪz/ to give /laɪkɪz/.

3 ◀)) 1.11 Listen and repeat the statements in 2, paying attention to the linking.

4 Complete the statements so that they are true for you.

   a A place I'd like to visit is _____

   b I've always enjoyed _____

   c I don't often eat _____

   d What I like about my home is _____

   e Learning English is _____

   f I've always wanted to _____

   g When I get up in the morning _____

5 Identify and mark the linking in the statements.

6 Practise saying the statements.

Exam listening

Section 1

 1.12

Questions 1–5

Complete the form below. Write **NO MORE THAN TWO WORDS OR A NUMBER** for each answer.

Wright's Employment Agency
Registration form

Name: Helen **0** ....*SHEPARD*........

Address: 18 Henley Street, Mill Town

Post code: **1** ....

Telephone: 07945 76674

Looking for **2** .... work.

Experience:

- **3** .... in residential children's home
- waitressing
- cleaning in hotel

Own transport? **4** ....

Availability: not night shifts, can start **5** ....

> ### Exam information
> The order of the numbers in the table indicates the order in which you will hear the information. Here, it indicates that you will hear each job described in turn.

 1.13

Questions 6–10

Complete the table below. Write **NO MORE THAN TWO WORDS OR A NUMBER** for each answer.

Job	Location	Hours	Hourly rate
Hylands Hotel (cleaning, waitressing, kitchen work)	Near **6**	Shift work No later than 10 pm	£6.75 plus **7** ....
The Cedars (home for elderly)	Hamilton Terrace	**8** .... Some weekends and evenings	£6.10
Looking after **9**	Poplar Street	2–3 hours each morning	**10** .... plus transport

2 Taste

UNIT AIMS

LISTENING SKILLS
Labelling a map or plan

SPEAKING SKILLS
Part 2: Describing an arts or media event
Using cleft sentences
Talking about likes and preferences

PRONUNCIATION
Sentence stress

EXAM LISTENING
Section 2

Topic talk

1 Look at the pictures and answer the questions below.

   a Do you follow the latest trends in fashion, music and technology?

   b How important is looking fashionable to you?

   c Do you have similar tastes to your friends and family?

   d Which of the fashions opposite would you prefer? Why?

2 Decide which adjective in the box best matches the descriptions (a–g) below.

> classic ■ conservative ■ contemporary ■ functional
> mainstream ■ over the top ■ retro ■ unique

Example
He prefers modern over traditional and follows the latest trends. ___*contemporary*___

   a He likes wearing fashions from the sixties and seventies.

   _____

   b I'm not sure I like her fashion sense – it's a little too dramatic and exaggerated for my taste. _____

   c I prefer simple, well-cut clothes that don't go out of fashion.

   _____

   d My parents are a little old-fashioned in their taste; they prefer traditional, plain designs. _____

   e I always think Italian women have a very distinctive style, unlike any other. _____

   f Nowadays it seems that almost everyone owns a least one pair of jeans.

   _____

   g The design of the house is simple and practical but not particularly attractive. _____

3 Choose two nouns from the box below which collocate with each of the adjectives in 2. Some of the adjectives may collocate with more than two nouns.

> a car ■ a design ■ a film ■ a haircut ■ fashion ■ music ■ an outfit ■ a room

4 Which of the adjectives in 2 best describes the following?

  a the design of your house/flat _____

  b the style of some of your family members _____

  c your taste in fashion _____

  d the style of your favourite actor or singer _____

  e the design of your workplace or place of study _____

5 Match each category (1–9) with the list of examples (a–i).

1 architecture	**a** a stand-up comedian, an opera, a ballet, a stage play
2 fashion	**b** a catwalk model, a designer label, a high street trend, a fashion designer
3 music	**c** a best-selling paperback, a classic novel, an historical biography, a collection of poetry
4 literature	**d** e-reader, a podcast, an internet blog, a social networking site
5 film	**e** an oil portrait, a watercolour landscape, a a sculpture, an abstract painting
6 visual arts	**f** a new release, a blockbuster, an art-house movie, a foreign language film
7 performing arts	**g** a broadsheet newspaper, a tabloid, a current affairs programme, a weekly magazine
8 traditional media	**h** a top ten hit, choral music, an orchestral piece, a cover version
9 new media	**i** high-rise apartments, a high-tech skyscraper, a building of historical interest, a slum

6 Think of some specific examples for some of the words in 5 and tell your partner.

Example
an opera: La Traviata

7 Complete the sentences below with an appropriate preposition. Some of the prepositions may be used more than once.

about ■ for ■ in ■ of ■ on ■ over ■ than ■ to

  a I'm not keen _____ choral music.

  b I am quite passionate _____ designer labels.

  c I can see the attraction _____ abstract art but it doesn't appeal _____ me at all.

  d I'm not a big fan _____ high street fashion.

  e I have a preference _____ classic novels _____ more contemporary ones.

  f I feel quite indifferent _____ most sculpture.

  g I have quite traditional tastes _____ music.

  h I would much rather watch an art-house film _____ a blockbuster.

  i I'm quite fond _____ ballet but don't care much _____ opera.

  j Tablets and e-readers are very much _____ fashion at the moment.

8 Which of the examples in 5 do you see, listen to or use regularly? Use the language in 7 to explain how you feel about them.

Listening skills

Labelling a map or plan

1 Look at the two plans. What does each one show? Which words gave you clues?

Plan A

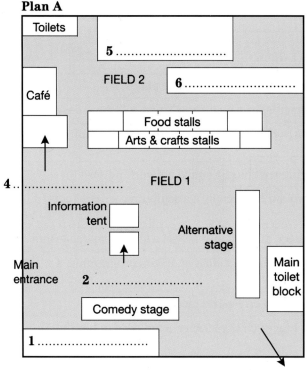

Plan B

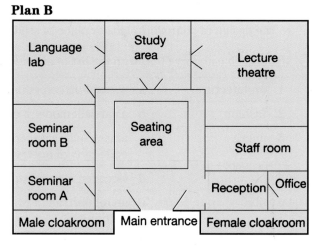

Exam information

In the Listening test, you may be asked to label a map or plan.
You will hear the answers in the same order as the questions.

2 Read the descriptions below and match them with locations 1–6 on plan A. Label the plan.

- The First Aid tent is directly in front of the main entrance next to the information tent.
- To get to the main stage, turn left at the entrance and head for the second field. You'll see the stage on the far side opposite the food stalls.
- The disabled toilets are in the first field not far from the entrance, in the corner behind the comedy stage.
- You'll find the children's play area in the second field, beside the café.
- Access to the camping area is in the far corner of the first field next to the main toilet block.
- The VIP area is at the far end of the second field directly opposite the café.

3 Look at the sentences (a–g) about plan B and decide if they are true or false.
If they are false, correct them.

a As you enter the department the seating area is directly in front of you. _____

b As you enter seminar room A the staff room is behind you. _____

c There are men's and women's cloakrooms on either side of the reception. _____

d As you come out of the lecture theatre the language lab is in front of you. _____

e From the office to seminar room B you need to cross the study area. _____

f To access the office you need to go through the lecture theatre. _____

g As you leave seminar room A, the men's cloakroom is on your right. _____

4 🔊 1.14 Listen to the receptionist describing three locations on Plan B. Which location is she describing in each case?

a _____

b _____

c _____

5 Practise describing different locations on the plans for your partner to find. Remember to state your current location in each case.

6 Look at the town plan below. What does it show?

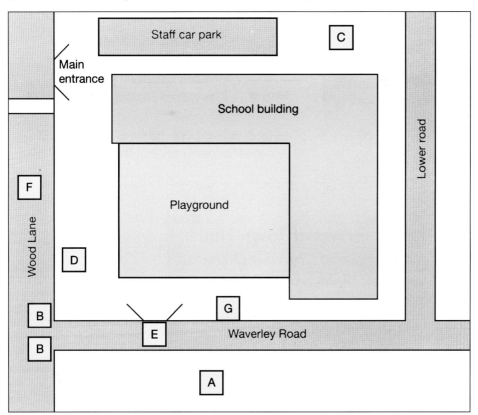

7 Before you listen, describe the locations of A–G on the map in relation to other places on the map.

Example
B is at the junction of Waverley Road and Wood Lane.

8 🔊 1.15 Listen to part of a recording and label the plan. Write the correct letter A–G next to questions 1–7 below.

1 Visitors' parking _____

2 Pedestrian crossing _____

3 Traffic calming _____

4 Traffic signs _____

5 New flats and offices _____

6 New fence _____

7 Garden _____

Speaking skills

Part 2: Describing an arts or media event

1 Look at the notices/adverts (A–C) and answer the questions below.

1 What type of event is each one advertising? _____

2 Have you been to any events like these recently? _____

3 Which of these events would you choose to go to? Why? _____

A

South Hill Arts Centre
Monday 5th–Sunday 18th October 10 am–4 pm
'Man and nature '
An exhibition exploring the human relationship
with the natural landscape featuring the work of
local photographer Henry Gregory.
Adults: £5
Free admission for under 12s and students.

B

Grangetown Dramatic Society
presents
A Midsummer Night's Dream
by William Shakespeare
Tuesday 5–Saturday 9 September
at The Priory Theatre Grangetown
Tickets available from Box Office 01856 875335

C

Netherwood Town Hall
Netherwood Chamber Orchestra
Mozart Violin concerto No 4
Mahler Symphony No 5
Friday 11 April 8 pm
Tickets £10, £7.50

2 1.16 Listen to a man talking about one of the events in 1. Which one is he describing? Did he enjoy it? Was there anything he didn't like?

Using cleft sentences

3 Complete the phrases the speaker uses to emphasize his points. Then listen again to check your answers.

a The thing _____ was the violin concerto.

b The _____ events like this is _____ I like to see local talent.

c What _____ how good amateur musicians can be.

d Something _____ was the age of the musicians.

e What _____ the venue.

Technique
To focus on a particular point and emphasize it, we often use a cleft sentence. These start with *The thing ...* , *Something ...* , *What ...* , *The reason why ...* and can be used to express how we feel about something using the verbs *like*, *dislike*, *love*, *hate*, *enjoy*, etc. For example: *The thing I liked most about the concert was the soloist.*

4 Rewrite these sentences using a cleft sentence starting with the prompt given.

Example
I especially loved his emotional performance.
Something that I especially loved was his emotional performance.
I didn't enjoy the concert because the sound quality was bad.
The reason why I didn't enjoy the concert was the sound quality was so bad.

a The small, intimate venue really made this show really special.

What _____

b The artist's talent really impressed me.

The thing _____

c I absolutely love her designs because they are so modern and fresh.

The reason _____

d I particularly remember the incredible costumes and scenery.

Something _____

e I'm not very keen on this type of modern art.

Something _____

f The fascinating story makes this film worth seeing.

The thing _____

g I didn't like the book because the story was so complicated.

The reason _____

h The film made me realize what difficult lives some people lead.

What _____

5 🔊 1.17 Listen and check your answers.

Talking about likes and preferences

6 Think about your own experience and choose one of the following.

> a cultural event ■ an exhibition ■ a film ■ a musical event ■ a play

Talk about
– why you went to the event
– what you enjoyed about it
– something that particularly impressed you about it
– one thing you didn't like about it.

Technique
To show emphasis, you can use adverbs like *really, especially, absolutely* and *particularly*.

7 Read the Speaking Part 2 task card below. Take one minute to think and make notes on the topic. Then practise speaking for two minutes on the topic.

> Describe an arts or entertainment event that you have attended.
>
> You should say
>
> – what kind of event it was
>
> – where it was held
>
> – what impression it had on you
>
> and explain whether or not you enjoyed it.

Pronunciation

Sentence stress

1 1.18 Listen to these speakers' impressions of different arts events. Underline the words that the speakers stress.

   a Something I really didn't like was the noise.
   b The thing I remember most is the beautiful choral piece.
   c What made the concert special was the fantastic choir.
   d What I absolutely loved about the play were the wonderful costumes.
   e The thing I particularly liked were the stunning visual effects.
   f The thing that really impressed me was the amazing script.

Technique

Speakers generally stress content words (words that carry meaning like nouns, verbs, adjectives and adverbs) rather than grammar words (prepositions, auxiliary verbs, pronouns, etc). However, any word may be stressed for emphasis.

2 Practise saying the sentences.

3 Look at the sentences below. Underline the words in each sentence that you think will be stressed.

   a I'm a big fan of contemporary art.
   b Orchestral music doesn't appeal to me at all.
   c I really can't see the attraction of the latest fashion trend.
   d I'm quite passionate about traditional dancing.
   e I'm not too keen on folk music but I love this song.
   f I absolutely love classic literature but I'm not too keen on this particular writer.

4 1.19 Listen and check your answers.

5 Rewrite the sentences in 3 so that they are true for you.

6 Practise saying the sentences.

Exam listening

Section 2

 1.20

Questions 11–15

*Choose the correct letter, **A**, **B** or **C**.*

11 The main purpose of the new Arts Centre is to provide

   A   entertainment and education opportunities

   B   education and local business opportunities

   C   entertainment and local business opportunities

12 Where can the permanent art exhibits be found?

   A   Exhibition Room A

   B   Exhibition Room B

   C   The Rees Gallery

13 The Drawing Workshop is for

   A   teenagers

   B   cartoonists

   C   local artists

14 The Youth Band and Choir are performing

   A   twice in the Gilbert Theatre

   B   at two different venues

   C   in the theatre and the Moffat Hall

15 The last event of the evening

   A   is in the Studio Theatre

   B   is a musical event

   C   is by a local performer

1.21

Questions 16–20.

*Label the plan below. Write **NO MORE THAN THREE WORDS** for each answer.*

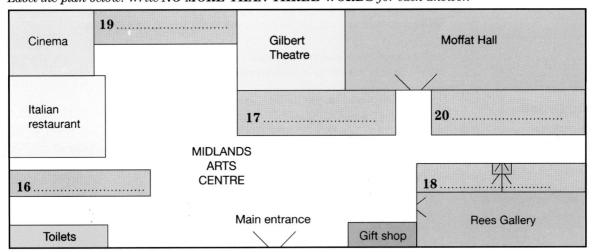

3 The world about us

LISTENING SKILLS
Identifying synonyms and paraphrases
Classification

SPEAKING SKILLS
Part 2: Describing something to help the environment
Part 3: Expressing views and opinions

PRONUNCIATION
Word stress in *-ion* nouns

EXAM LISTENING
Section 3

Topic talk

Waters rage as deluge continues

Heat wave nightmare

Hurricane wreaks devastation

1 Read the headlines and answer the questions.
  a What world issue do the three headlines represent?
  b Which parts of the world have experienced any of these in recent years?
  c What were the consequences?

2 Which of the following could be classified as natural disasters? Which could be caused by human activity?
  a civil war
  b drought
  c an earthquake
  d famine
  e flooding
  f a volcanic eruption

3 What are the possible causes and consequences of the issues in 1?
Make statements using the verbs in the box and the ideas below.
Example
An earthquake can lead to a tsunami.
Famine can be caused by a poor harvest.

> ### Technique
> Use modal verbs like *can, could, may* and *might* to avoid being too direct or definite. This is very common in academic writing as well as speaking.

can be affected by ■ can be caused by ■ can lead to can result in ■ can result from

  – climate change
  – deforestation
  – disease
  – economic crisis
  – endangered species
  – an epidemic

  – extreme temperatures
  – fossil fuel emissions
  – global warming
  – homelessness
  – a poor harvest

  – migration
  – poverty
  – refugees
  – a tsunami
  – unemployment

4 Choose the adjective in the following sentences which does NOT collocate with the noun that follows.

a Many people believe that global warming has caused *long-term/ irreversible/disastrous* damage to the environment.

b The situation is quickly deteriorating and could soon become a *widespread/major/humanitarian* disaster.

c Recent storms and flooding have caused *long-term/widespread/main* damage to the region.

d After the earthquake, many countries provided *emergency/disastrous/ financial* aid.

e The *ongoing/impending/trivial* crisis has caused many people to flee the country.

f It is feared that the disaster will have *far-reaching/eternal/environmental* consequences.

g The region is suffering a(n) *complicated/ongoing/humanitarian* crisis caused by the civil war.

h The recent extreme weather has had a(n) *important/devastating/ disastrous* effect on the local population.

5 Read the questions below. Which two questions are different from the others? In what way?

a What's the climate like in your country?

b How has the climate changed in recent years?

c What can individuals do to protect the environment?

d Do you believe businesses do enough to protect the environment?

e How will climate change affect people's lives in the future?

f Does it often snow in your country?

g What are some of the causes of water pollution?

h What consequences can a shortage of rain have on people's lives?

i What are the differences between old and young people's attitudes towards protecting the environment?

6 Which questions (a–i) in 5 require the following type of answers?

1 an explanation _____   **4** a personal opinion _____

2 a comparison _____   **5** a prediction _____

3 a suggestion or recommendation _____   **6** a personal experience _____

7 Match the answer types (1–6) in 6 with the phrases (a–j) below.

a It is quite likely that _____

b The main difference is _____

c They should definitely _____

d We tend to have a lot of _____

e Personally, I think _____

f It would be a good idea if _____

g There are now far more _____

h There will probably be _____

i Very rarely, but last year we _____

j There are several negative effects including _____

k In my view, _____

8 With a partner, ask and answer the questions in 5. Start your answers by using some of the phrases in 7.

Listening skills

Identifying synonyms and paraphrases

1 Look at the following exam questions. Can you think of different ways of expressing the information in the answer options (a–c)?

> **Exam information**
>
> In the Listening test the audio recording and the question may use different words to talk about the same point by either using synonyms (words which have the same or similar meaning) or paraphrasing (rewording a phrase or idea).

1 The lecture is being given by

   a a writer

   b a lecturer

   c a postgraduate student

2 Mel and Andrew agree to meet at

   a 1.30 pm

   b 1.45 pm

   c 2.30 pm

3 Mel and Andrew agree to meet in

   a the canteen

   b a café

   c the Science building

2 ◀》1.22 Listen to two students talking about a lecture and answer the questions.

3 Look at the audio script or listen again and find any paraphrases or synonyms of the answers.

> **Exam information**
>
> In Speaking Part 2 you may be asked to talk about an experience or event in your life. Use adjectives to describe the event and how it made you feel.

4 Read the questions for the next part of the conversation. Underline the key words and think of possible synonyms or paraphrases.

4 Mel was surprised at the speaker's .... theories.

5 Mrs McKee did not have any .... to support her argument about sea levels.

6 Mel plans to follow Mrs McKee's ....

5 ◀》1.23 Listen to the students talking after the lecture and complete sentences 4–6 in 4. Use NO MORE THAN TWO WORDS for each answer.

Classification

> **Exam information**
>
> In classification questions you will be given a list of options (labelled A, B and C.) from which to choose, and numbered questions. As you listen you will have to match the questions to one of options. You can choose an option more than once. The questions will appear in the same order as you hear the answers.

6 Questions 1–6 show events in the history of climate change. Use your own knowledge of the subject to predict during which periods (A–C) they occurred.

> **Technique**
>
> Try to think of synonyms or paraphrase the options and/or the questions.

- **A** 19th century
- **B** mid 20th century
- **C** 1970s–80s

1 The term *the greenhouse effect* was invented. _____

2 Average temperatures started to increase considerably. _____

3 There was a decrease in average temperatures for a few years _____

4 Methane and nitrous oxide were first identified as greenhouse gases. _____

5 Carbon dioxide was first identified as a greenhouse gas. _____

6 Many high temperature records were broken. _____

7 A major drought occurred in North America. _____

7 Underline any key words in the questions and options. Try to paraphrase or think of synonyms for each of the questions and options.

8 1.24 Listen to the dialogue and classify the events as A, B or C.

Speaking skills

1 Read the 12 ideas below on how to save the planet and answer questions a and b below.

   a How often do you do the following activities? (always, regularly, occasionally, never?)

12 ways to save the planet

   1 Walk or ride a bike to work/place of study.
   2 Recycle glass, paper, aluminium, etc.
   3 Compost food waste.
   4 Switch off electrical items like computers at night.
   5 Turn off lights when you're not in the room.
   6 Have a shower rather than a bath.
   7 Buy locally grown produce.
   8 Donate unwanted items to charity.
   9 Buy clothes, furniture or other items second hand.
10 Take your own bags to the supermarket.
11 Bank and pay bills online.
12 Have a vegetarian meal.

   b How can doing these activities help save the planet? If people didn't do any of them, how might this affect the planet? Use some of the verbs and nouns below to help you.

Example
Walking to work saves fuel consumption and reduces carbon emissions.

> add to ■ conserve ■ contribute to ■ recycle
> save ■ reduce ■ use ■ waste

> air miles ■ carbon emissions ■ carbon footprint ■ energy (consumption)
> fuel (consumption) ■ money ■ landfill ■ water (consumption)

Part 2: Describing something to help the environment

2 Read the task card below. Take one minute to prepare and make notes. Then spend two minutes talking about the topic.

> Describe something you do to help the environment.
>
> You should say
>
> – what it is you do
>
> – how you do it
>
> – how often you do it
>
> – and explain in what way your action helps the environment.

Part 3: Expressing views and opinions

3 Complete the sentences (1–8) with the words below.

against ■ agree ■ believe ■ far ■ me ■ tend ■ view ■ would

1 Most people would _____ that it is essential for big companies to reduce their carbon emissions.

2 As _____ as I can see, the problems caused by fossil fuel emissions and deforestation are not going to disappear.

3 For _____ , fuel emissions from cars are one of the biggest sources of air pollution.

4 I _____ to think that some claims about climate change and extreme weather are exaggerated.

5 I'm totally _____ the amount of plastic packaging most manufacturers use for their products.

6 I _____ say that companies found to be contaminating rivers and the sea should be heavily fined.

7 In my _____ , the increase in the number of endangered species is a real cause for concern.

8 I don't _____ that some individuals are aware of how serious some of these environmental issues are.

4 Match the justifications (a–h) below with the opinions (1–8) in 3.

a Unless they take action, there could be severe consequences for future generations. _____

b I'm more concerned about economic issues and global poverty and starvation. _____

c That's why it's so important to educate people, particularly children, so that they grow up with a good understanding of how to protect our planet from total destruction. _____

d If more people left their vehicles at home and walked or shared lifts, this would be greatly reduced. _____

e Although some governments and businesses have taken measures to deal with these issues, I don't think they have gone far enough. _____

f That's why I am a big supporter of charities that support animal and plant conservation. _____

g This already happens in my country and it has greatly reduced the amount of water pollution in recent years. _____

h I don't think it's necessary and not only is it a waste of money, it also adds to landfill. _____

Technique
When expressing an opinion it is important to support and justify your view.

Pronunciation

Word stress in *-ion* nouns

1 The following verbs and nouns all appear in this unit. Complete the table with the corresponding noun or verb.

Verb	Noun	Verb	Noun
exaggerate		protect	
	pollution		information
justify		conserve	
	consumption		presentation
contribute		realize	
	destruction		population
deteriorate		prevent	
	emission		migration
contaminate		reduce	
	classification		recommendation

2 ◀» 1.25 Mark the stress on the verbs and nouns. Listen and check. Can you see a pattern in the position of the stressed syllable in the nouns?

3 Complete the questions with one of the words from the table in 1. There may be more than one possible answer.

   a What type of human activity _____ to global warming?

   b What effect does the _____ of the rainforest have on wildlife?

   c How can a _____ in air quality affect people's health?

   d How can households reduce their water _____ ?

   e Has the _____ in your home town increased or decreased in recent years?

   f Does your country experience economic _____ from other countries?

   g What is the best way for individuals to _____ their local environment?

   h How can you _____ supporting animal charities when so many humans live in poverty?

4 With a partner, ask and answer the questions.

Exam listening

Section 3

 1.26

Question 21

*Choose the correct letter, **A**, **B** or **C**.*

21 Why was the tutor initially concerned about the Mel's choice of subject?

A There was not enough information on the subject.

B The subject was not new or different.

C Mel had taken a different approach to the subject.

Questions 22–25

*Write the correct letter, **A**, **B** or **C** next to questions 22–25.*

Mel should

A include it

B remove it

C increase it

22 the introduction _____

23 statistics about flooding _____

24 acknowledgement of visual material _____

25 a graph about rainfall _____

1.27

Questions 26–30

Complete the flow chart.

*Write **NO MORE THAN TWO WORDS OR A NUMBER** for each answer.*

Advice on presentation
Be well prepared with content and equipment.

⇩

Prepare slides with main points and visuals.
No bright colours, **26** .... or sound effects.

⇩

Stand in a central position.
Make **27** .... with audience.
Use a **28** .... mouse or keyboard.

⇩

Speak slowly.
Don't memorize or read.
Use cue cards as a **29** ....

⇩

Deal with **30** .... from audience at end.

4

Language and communication

UNIT AIMS

LISTENING SKILLS
Visual multiple choice
Table completion

SPEAKING SKILLS
Part 3: Agreeing and disagreeing
Part 2: Making notes

PRONUNCIATION
Word linking 2

EXAM LISTENING
Section 4

Topic talk

1 Look at the picture and answer the questions.

  a How long have you been learning English?

  b What for you is the most difficult thing about learning English?

  c Have you learnt any other foreign languages apart from English?

  d How important is it to learn a foreign language?

  e What is the most effective way to learn a language?

2 Complete the opinions (a–j) with a word from the box.

> common ■ dead ■ face-to-face ■ first ■ cross-cultural
> minority ■ non-verbal ■ official ■ second ■ written

  a _____ languages will die out unless people make an effort to protect them.

  b If English is your _____ language, you will have greater opportunities in life.

  c The reason people can find _____ communication difficult is due to different behaviour and values rather than the language barrier.

  d _____ communication using technology like video conferencing and webcam is the same as talking to someone in the flesh.

  e When nations share a _____ language, they are likely to have good relations.

  f Children who are taught a _____ language from an early age are far more likely to become fluent.

  g There is no point in learning a _____ language like Latin.

  h The decline in the standards of _____ communication and literacy skills in general is due to an increase in text messaging and social networking amongst young people.

  i All citizens of a country should be forced to learn the _____ language even if it is not their mother tongue.

  j Body language, facial expression and other _____ communication skills are more important than speech in conveying emotions.

3 The phrases below could be used to agree or disagree with the statements in 1. Decide which phrases (a–h) express the following.

strong agreement _____

cautious agreement _____

cautious disagreement _____

strong disagreement _____

a I'm not sure I agree with that.
b I agree up to a point.
c I sure that's not right.
d Personally, I'd say the opposite.
e I agree to some extent
f I would tend to agree.
g I couldn't agree more.
h There's no doubt about it.
i That's so true.
j I'm not so sure about that.

4 Match the responses (1–10) below with the statements (a–j) in 2.

1 There are plenty of examples in history which show that this is not true and it is often neighbouring states who speak the same or similar languages who end up at war. However, I do think that a shared language can help strengthen ties in some cases. _____

2 Even if you speak the same language, cultural differences can cause significant misunderstandings between people and can lead to a total breakdown in communication. _____

3 Governments should do far more to ensure these languages are taught in schools because we rely on the younger generations to keep them alive for the future. _____

4 I think everyone should be able to communicate at a basic level in the official language but they should also be free to use their own language whenever they want. _____

5 But it all depends on how well you are taught. Many people learn a language at primary school but they don't all go on to speak it fluently. _____

6 I think a knowledge of English can be very useful for work and study but it doesn't necessarily have to be your mother tongue. I think it is more useful to be able to speak a number of languages well than to speak only English. _____

7 You can tell far more about how someone is feeling from how he communicates than from what he actually says. _____

8 It's not the same as being in the same room with someone – there is always going to be a slight barrier if you are speaking to someone on a screen. _____

9 It can really help if you are a linguist as so many other languages have their roots in Latin, so it's great for understanding vocabulary. And like any academic subject it is good mental exercise. _____

10 Spelling and punctuation in particular have really deteriorated and it can only be because young people are so used to using abbreviated text language. _____

> **Technique**
>
> In Part 3 of the Speaking test, you may be asked whether you agree or disagree with an opinion. Remember, there is no right or wrong answer but you must be able to justify your opinion.

5 Decide if the response is showing agreement or disagreement and choose a suitable phrase (a–h) from 3 to start the response.

6 Do you agree or disagree with the opinions in 2? Talk to your partner.

Listening skills

Visual multiple choice

1 Look at the three multiple choice questions in 2 from a Section 4 listening about languages and answer the questions (a–d).

> **Exam information**
>
> Section 4 of the Listening test is a monologue or lecture on an academic topic. There are at least two question types. The questions may give important clues about the content and structure of the talk.

   a In which area of the world are the languages spoken?

   b Is the subject of the lecture rare or common languages? How can you tell?

   c Look at the map in question 1. Which areas are shaded? If you do not know the name of the country or region, how could you describe the region geographically?

   d Look at the three bar charts in questions 2 and 3. What figures do you think each one shows?

2 ◀)) 1.28 Listen to the first part of the lecture and answer the questions. Choose the correct letter, A, B or C.

   1 Which area represents the languages the lecturer will concentrate on?

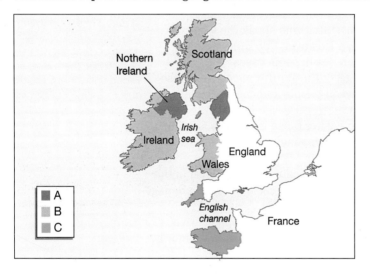

   2 Which chart represents the number of speakers of Breton?

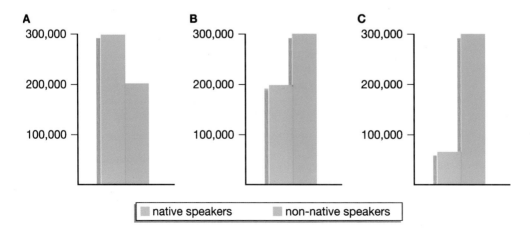

3 Which chart represents the number of speakers of Manx?

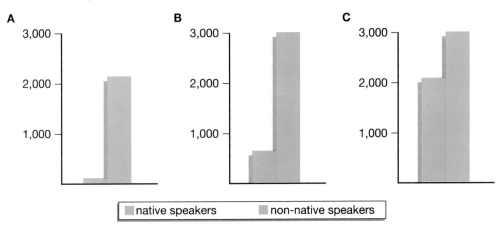

Table completion

3 Look at the table below for the second part of the lecture and answer the questions below.

a What information will the lecturer talk about next?
b What does the numbering of the questions tell you about the order in which you will hear the information?
c Predict the type of information that is needed to complete each gap.

4 ◀)) 1.29 Listen and complete questions 4–10.

Complete the table below.
Write NO MORE THAN THREE WORDS AND/OR A NUMBER for each answer.

	Decline	Revival	Official status	UNESCO status
Cornish	Rapid decline since peak in **4**	– Started early 20th century – Publications, films and music – Taught in some schools	Recognized as UK **5** .... in 2002	Critically endangered language (revitalized)
Manx	**6** .... died in 1974	– Taught as second language in schools – **7** .... on island – Radio broadcasts in Manx	Recognized as Isle of Man's official language in 1985	Critically endangered (revitalized)
Breton	Large decrease in numbers in **8** .... of 20th century	– Breton language-medium schools – Large body of literature and media	**9** .... as official language due to French Constitution	**10** ....

Speaking skills

Part 3: Agreeing and disagreeing

1 Look at the list of ways of communicating.

  a Which do you use on a regular (daily) basis?

  b Which do you use regularly but not every day?

  c Which did you used to use more regularly than you do now?

  d Which do you think you will not use as much in the future?

  e Which have you never used?

- text messaging
- telephone calls from a landline
- telephone calls on a mobile
- handwritten letters
- fax
- email
- typed or word-processed letters
- social networking
- instant messaging

2 What are the benefits and drawbacks of each type of communication in 1?
Use the ideas below to help you.

Example
*Text messaging is a convenient and immediate form of communication but it can be
too informal for some situations and messages can be deleted very easily.*

– easy to use	– behind the times
– convenient	– interactive
– public	– temporary
– time-consuming	– confidential
– personal	– slow
– costly	– impersonal
– immediate	– formal
– easily deleted	– harmful
– permanent	– informal

Part 2: Making notes

3 Read the Part 2 task card below and answer the questions.

  a What is the main topic?

  b What tense are you expected to use for the most part?

> Describe an important letter you received.
>
> You should say
>
> – who it was from
>
> – when you received it
>
> – what it was about
>
> and explain why it was important to you.

4 1.30 Listen to a candidate doing the task. As you listen, note down what he says about each of the main points on the task card. Write only the important points.

Example
Who it was from: boss

5 Listen again. What extra details does he add?

Example
formal letter, interview a few weeks before

6 Look at the notes that the candidate wrote to prepare for the same task. Did the candidate mention all the points on the card? How similar are the notes to the ones you made as you listened?

— boss — formal letter — job offer

— last April, long wait after interview, thought it was rejection

— short, start date, pay, invite to HR dept

— first job — pleased, wanted job, surprised, excited

7 Read the task card below and answer the questions.
   a What is the main topic?
   b What tense are you expected to use for the most part?

Talk about a person you regularly communicate with but don't often see.
You should say
   – who the person is
   – how you communicate with them
   – what you communicate about
and explain why communication with this person is important to you.

8 Take one minute to prepare. Make a note of the main ideas and key words first. Then in the remaining time add any details. Use your notes to speak for two minutes on the topic.

Technique
You will be given one minute to prepare for your talk so use this time wisely. Make notes of the main points and key vocabulary and refer to these as you talk to help you remember.

Pronunciation

Word linking 2

1 🔊 1.31 Listen to the following extracts from the Speaking task on page 35. Complete the extracts with TWO WORDS in each gap.

a I'd like to talk about a _____ received last year.

b I had been _____ interview a few weeks before ...

c I remember _____ to my family that I hadn't got it ...

d I almost didn't _____ reading it!

e The _____ was quite short.

f What I remember most is being _____ as it was my first job offer ...

Technique

When one word ends in a vowel sound and the following word starts with a vowel sound, we often link the two together by adding an extra 'intruding' sound. The intrusive sounds are /j/, /r/ and /w/.

---

2 Listen again. There is an extra sound linking the two words together. What is the extra sound in each case? Practise saying the extracts, paying particular attention to the linking.

3 Identify and mark the intrusive sounds in the questions below, as in the example.

a How often do you check your email inbox?

Do you think this is too often?

b Are there any minority languages in your country?

Are they in danger of extinction?

c How effective are your oral communication skills? What can you do to improve them?

d Does mobile technology make it easier or more difficult to switch off from study or work?

e Is your own language difficult for other language speakers to learn?

f How are languages best learnt? Are they easier to learn when you are young?

4 🔊 1.32 Listen to the questions in 3 and repeat them.

5 With a partner, ask and answer the questions.

Exam listening

Section 4

 1.33

Questions 31–37

*Choose the correct letter, **A**, **B** or **C**.*

31 Which pie chart shows the percentage of people who make a phone call every day?

A   B   C

47%

92%

53%

32 Which pie chart shows the percentage of young people who text every day?

A   B   C

15%

90%

65%

33 On average men

  A   send fewer texts than women

  B   send shorter texts than women

  C   have fewer contacts than women

34 Originally, text messaging was created as

  A   an internal messaging system

  B   a new commercial venture for a mobile phone company

  C   a way of sending greetings to friends and family

35 Early texters were limited by

  A   incompatibility between mobile phone networks

  B   unsophisticated mobile phones

  C   expensive mobile phones

36 Abbreviated texting language

  A   is unpopular with many people

  B   was created due to limitations in text length

  C   has caused children's language skills to decline

37 On average, children who text

  A   have better speaking skills than those who don't

  B   have better reading and writing skills than those who don't

  C   do not show any difference in their language skills

 1.34

Questions 38–40

*Choose **THREE** letters A–G.*

Which three uses of text messaging were mentioned in the survey?

A   taking part in a competition

B   booking a hotel room

C   buying an airline ticket

D   following a package delivery

E   making a doctor's appointment

F   making a donation

G   voting in an election

5 Food for thought

UNIT AIMS

LISTENING SKILLS
Nominalization in paraphrasing
Sentence completion

SPEAKING SKILLS
Part 3: Asking for clarification and giving
yourself thinking time

PRONUNCIATION
Weak forms of auxiliary verbs

EXAM LISTENING
Section 2

Topic talk

1 Look at the pictures and answer the questions.

  a Which of the eating situations can you most relate to?
  b Where do you eat on an average day? Who do you eat with?
  c Do you think your eating habits are generally healthy or unhealthy?

2 Which of the following statements are examples of healthy habits? Which are unhealthy? Which could be either? Which are true for you?

  1 I try to avoid eating late at night.
  2 I'm always eating on the go.
  3 I make a real effort to have a proper sit-down meal every day.
  4 I tend to eat a lot of snacks like chocolate and crisps.
  5 I rarely cook for myself.
  6 I eat out at least once a week.
  7 I often skip breakfast in the morning.
  8 I try to eat fresh fruit and vegetables every day.

3 Match the reasons below (a–h) with the statements in 2 (1–8).

  a I just don't feel hungry first thing so I usually just have a coffee to keep me going. _____
  b I always carry a supply in my bag. I'm lucky that I don't put on weight easily. _____
  c I don't know how to. My flat mate is a brilliant cook so he always cooks for me. _____
  d I think you're supposed to eat five a day to keep healthy. _____
  e It makes a change to cooking every night. _____
  f It's important to take time over a meal and spend time with your family. _____
  g I just don't have time to sit down for a meal so I just grab a quick snack. _____
  h I find it stops me sleeping well and I don't think it's good for your digestion. _____

4 Choose examples from the box of foods which are high in the food properties (a–g) below. Some foods fit into more than one category

> berries ■ butter ■ citrus fruit ■ chocolate ■ eggs ■ fizzy drinks ■ green vegetables
> lentils ■ liver ■ nuts ■ oily fish ■ pasta ■ rice ■ ready meals ■ wholemeal bread

    a carbohydrates _____

    b protein_____

    c fibre _____

    d vitamins and minerals _____

    e cholesterol _____

    f additives, e.g. colourings and preservatives _____

    g calories _____

5 Add one more example of your own to each list.

6 Complete the sentences below about health problems caused by diet with nouns from the box.

> food poisoning ■ heart disease ■ high blood pressure ■ hyperactivity
> indigestion ■ malnutrition ■ obesity ■ tooth decay

    a It is thought that the recent outbreak of _____ was caused by contaminated or improperly cooked food.

    b Some parents avoid foods high in additives as they believe they can cause

       _____ in children.

    c It is generally believed that a diet high in salt can lead to _____ .

    d _____ is a result of poor oral hygiene and too many high-sugar foods and drinks.

    e A fatty diet can lead to high levels of cholesterol which may in turn lead to

       _____ .

    f Some people find that eating too much rich spicy food can give them

       _____ .

    g A poor diet with a lack of sufficient nutrients may result in

       _____ .

    h The most common causes of_____ are a diet high in fat and sugar and a lack of exercise.

7 What are the benefits of eating the following types of food? What are the drawbacks? Give reasons and examples for your answers.

    a vegetarian or vegan food

    b low-fat foods

    c organic fruit and vegetables

    d free-range meat and eggs

Listening skills

Nominalization in paraphrasing

1 Read the short texts below and answer the questions.

A

> Nowadays the variety and availability of food means there is far more customer choice than half a century ago. However, global population growth and increasing environmental concerns have led to doubts about the long-term feasibility of maintaining supplies of basic foodstuffs. This has resulted in increased research into new foods and farming methods.

B

These days we can get so many different types of food – there is a lot more for customers to choose from than there was 50 years ago. But because the world population is growing and there are so many more problems with the environment, people are worried that we won't be able to keep on feeding everyone in the future. That's why scientists are looking into new types of food and the way farmers grow their crops.

a Which text is more informal? Which is more formal and academic?
b Which text uses more noun phrases?
Underline examples of noun phrases which are used to replace verbs.

Technique

Nominalization is the use of a noun or noun phrase to replace a verb. It is commonly used in academic writing but you will also find it used to paraphrase in IELTS Listening questions.

2 Paraphrase the following sentences using nominalization.

a Obesity is increasing rapidly and doctors are becoming concerned.

_____

b Farming methods have developed which produce more crops.

_____

c Eating plenty of oily fish can increase concentration levels.

_____

d People who don't eat meat may not have enough protein in their diet.

_____

e More and more young people take extreme measures to lose weight.

_____

f People are more interested in foreign cuisine so it is easier to find
unusual ingredients in supermarkets.

_____

Sentence completion

3 Read the sentence completion questions (1–4) and underline the key words.

WRITE **_NO MORE THAN THREE WORDS OR A NUMBER_** for
each answer.

1 Children who have a poor diet have an inferior ....

2 Other factors looked at include maternal age and ....

3 Children with an unhealthy diet suffer from a lack of ....

4 Rapid brain growth declines at the age of ....

4 The sentences are written in a formal, academic style with an emphasis on noun
phrases (_a poor diet, maternal age, a lack of, rapid brain growth_)
How might they be different in spoken English?

5 1.35 Listen and complete the sentences in 3.

6 Look at the audio script on page 101. Underline the paraphrases of the questions.

Speaking skills

Part 3 : Asking for clarification and giving yourself thinking time

1 Read the following opinions about food and diet. Which statements do you agree with and which do you disagree with? Why? Tell your partner.

   a Extreme diets don't work and can be dangerous.
   b People who have more food choices tend to have less healthy diets.
   c If you follow a healthy diet there is no need to take extra vitamins and minerals.
   d A diet without meat is unnatural; we need meat to be strong and healthy.
   e A rise in food allergies is due to environmental factors.
   f Our modern-day eating habits are healthier than they were 100 years ago.
   g There is no point in providing food aid to poor nations.
   h Cooking should be a compulsory subject for all children.

2 The statements in 1 were all made in response to Part 3 questions. Match the questions (1–8) with the statements (a–h) above.

   1 Do you think people in western countries have health problems that are related to food? _____

   2 How are eating habits now different from eating habits in the past? _____

   3 What is the safest way to lose weight? _____

   4 Do you think children should be taught how to cook at school? _____

   5 Do you think a vegetarian diet can be healthy? _____

   6 What can be done to prevent famine in poor countries? _____

   7 Why do you think there are now more people who have an allergic reaction to some foods? _____

   8 How do you feel about dietary supplements? _____

3 The statements below extend the opinions in 1. Match the extensions (1–8) to the opinions (a–h) in 1.

   1 Unfortunately not all parents teach their children to cook, so they should have classes in food and nutrition at school. _____

   2 There's a lot more pollution around now which means we are breathing air that isn't clean and drinking water that's been purified artificially. _____

   3 It's much better to lose weight slowly over a period of time – that way you can maintain the weight loss. _____

   4 It would be more effective to teach the people there how to produce food for themselves. _____

   5 More people around the world are more prosperous now than in the past, which means they can afford to eat better. _____

   6 It depends on whether you only avoid meat – many vegetarians don't eat fish or dairy products either.

   7 It's healthier to eat foods that contain those elements. _____

   8 It seems that being able to choose lots of different foods makes us forget the need to have a balanced diet. _____

4 Read the following further statements about food and diet. What questions do you think the examiner asked to produce these answers?

1 I'm worried that it encourages teenagers to try to lose weight when they don't need to, and it's about making a profit rather than promoting healthy eating habits.

_____

2 A balanced diet is essential in order to stay healthy, and understanding which foods contain carbohydrates, fat, protein and so on helps us to maintain healthy eating habits.

_____

3 It's probably because of the type of crops that traditionally grew there, but modern farming methods make it possible to grow anything in any climate.

_____

4 The world is running out of food and we have an expanding population, so we will have to find a way of producing food that provides us with the nutrients we need more efficiently.

_____

5 Treating food as fuel encourages us to eat processed food that can be eaten quickly, instead of taking time to eat fresh food properly prepared and cooked.

_____

5 1.36–1.39 Listen to four candidates answering some of the questions from 2. Match the speaker to the correct question.

Speaker 1: _____

Speaker 2: _____

Speaker 3: _____

Speaker 4: _____

Technique

If you have difficulty understanding the question or thinking of ideas, try to clarify what the examiner wants or use a phrase to give yourself thinking time.

---

6 Listen again and write down any phrases the speakers use to ask for clarification and give themselves thinking time.

Asking for clarification:

_____

Gaining thinking time:

_____

7 With a partner, think of further expressions for asking for clarification and gaining thinking time.

Asking for clarification:

_____

Gaining thinking time:

_____

8 With a partner, ask and answer the questions in 2.

Pronunciation

Weak forms of auxiliary verbs

1 Read the task card below. Tell your partner about a special meal you have had recently.

> Describe a special meal you had recently.
>
> You should say
>
> – what the meal was
> – where you had it
> – who you were with
>
> and explain what was the significance or importance of the meal.

2 🔊 1.40 Listen to six extracts from a candidate doing the task in 1 and write the missing verbs in the gaps.

a I_____ to tell you about a special meal I _____ recently.

b It_____ my birthday and my friends _____ a surprise evening out for me.

c It_____ a restaurant I _____ to go to ever since it _____ so I_____ very excited.

d We_____ there before so we _____ sure what to expect but we _____ it _____ very good.

e For my main course, I _____ lasagne, which _____ a dish _____many times before, but this one _____ absolutely outstanding.

f I   just _____ that they _____ in a few weeks' time to redecorate but I think they _____ again by New Year.

3 Listen again. Which of the verbs are stressed? Which are unstressed or weak?

4 Underline the auxiliary verbs in the sentences below. Practise saying the sentences, paying attention to the weak forms.

a I'll have been there by then.
b I've been looking forward to going there.
c I was told to order the fish.
d We were given a free drink.
e I've never been there before.
f They're offering a discount.
g I wasn't sure what they were doing.
h I'd like to have been there.

> ### Technique
> Main verbs are strong (stressed). Auxiliary verbs (*be, have, do*) and modal auxiliary verbs (*can, will, must, would,* etc) are generally weak except in negatives and short answers, or when used for emphasis. Remember that the auxiliary verbs *have* and *do* can also function as main verbs, in which case they will be strong.

Exam listening

Section 2

 1.41

Questions 11–15

Complete the sentences below.

Use **NO MORE THAN THREE WORDS AND/OR A NUMBER** *for each answer.*

Castle Hotel Food Lovers' Weekend

11 The chef will show participants how to make some ....

12 The cookery demonstration starts at ....

13 The museum entrance fee is ....

14 The seafood dinner starts at ....

15 The evening's entertainment is provided by an ....

 1.42

Questions 16–18

*Choose **THREE** letters **A–G**.*

Which three activities will participants be able to do on the culinary tour?

A   go shopping

B   see a photography exhibition

C   have an oyster lunch

D   go for a walk before lunch

E   make butter

F   watch a baking demonstration

G   make cakes

H   go on a fishing trip

Questions 19 and 20

*Choose **TWO** letters **A–E**.*

Which two activities can participants choose to do on Monday morning?

A   a talk from a cookery writer

B   a museum visit

C   a cookery demonstration

D   a trip to a market

E   a visit to a castle

Science
and technology

UNIT AIMS

LISTENING SKILLS
Identifying and avoiding distractors
Matching

SPEAKING SKILLS
Part 3: Making generalizations

PRONUNCIATION
Sounding interested

EXAM LISTENING
Section 4

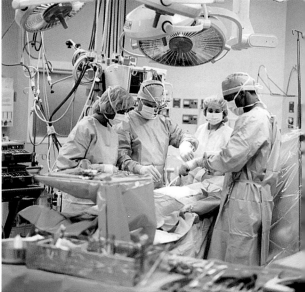

Topic talk

1 Look at the pictures and answer the questions below.

   a What role do scientists and engineers play in the situations in the pictures?

   b To which other areas of life do scientists and engineers contribute?

   c What skills and qualities do you need to be a scientist or an engineer?

2 Match the branches of science (1–10) with the area each one involves (a–j).

1	biology	**a**	forces and energy in the world around us
2	chemistry	**b**	chemical elements, their compounds and how they react
3	physics		
4	psychology	**c**	the earth's atmosphere and weather
5	botany	**d**	the mind and its effect on behaviour
6	astronomy	**e**	society and how human beings behave in groups
7	sociology	**f**	plants, animals and all living things
8	geology	**g**	the structure and materials of the earth, e.g. rocks and minerals
9	meteorology		
10	ecology	**h**	the environment and the things that live in it
		i	plants
		j	the stars, planets and galaxies

3 Do you study or you have studied any of these sciences? Do you plan to study any of them in the future?

4 Which branch of science would you describe in the following ways? Give reasons for your answers.

  a the most interesting
  b of the most practical use
  c the most difficult to study
  d of the most relevance today

5 What are the adjectives for each of the nouns in 2?

  Example
  biology: biological

6 How have engineers and scientists contributed to the following areas of life? Think of at least one example for each area.

  a buildings and homes
  b communication
  c food and agriculture
  d health and medicine
  e natural disasters
  f travel and transport
  g work
  h power and energy

7 Look at the list of scientific and engineering achievements (a–j). Match the achievements to the examples (1–10).

  a water supply and distribution
  b imaging
  c agricultural mechanization
  d household appliances
  e high-performance materials
  f roads
  g electrification
  h electronics
  i health technologies
  j the motor car

  1 cardiac pacemaker, kidney dialysis machine, laser surgery
  2 stainless steel, nylon, carbon fibre
  3 hydraulic brakes, electronic fuel injection system, airbags
  4 the transistor, the microprocessor, the integrated circuit
  5 railways, light bulbs, domestic heating systems
  6 tractors, the internal combustion engine, the combine harvester
  7 canals, desalination plants, pipes
  8 radar, photography, ultrasound
  9 the washing machine, the dishwasher, the vacuum cleaner
  10 motorways, tarmac, Catseyes

8 Number each achievement (a–j) in 7 according to how important you consider it. (1 = least important, 10 = most important).

9 Compare lists with another student. Explain the reasons for your choices.

  Example
  I think electronics are important because they contribute to so many other things.
  Without them we wouldn't have computers, mobile phones or TVs.

Listening skills

Identifying and avoiding distractors

Technique
A distractor is a key word used in the listening which is specifically designed to distract you and lead you to an incorrect answer.

1 Read the following multiple choice question and answer questions a and b.

> Dan got the idea for his research from
>
> **A** a friend of his tutor's
>
> **B** a postgraduate student in his department
>
> **C** an article he read in a scientific journal

a What are the key words in the question? Underline them.
b Can you think of any synonyms for the key words?

2 Read the audio script below of part of the listening task to find the answer to 1.

a What is the correct answer? _____

b Underline the distractors. What information tells you that the distractors are incorrect?

Dan I've been doing some research into the popularity of engineering as a university subject and in particular the number of females choosing this subject. My main research was based on UK home students but I wanted to make a comparison with international students in the UK and with students studying engineering in other countries.

First, a little about my reasons for choosing this area of research. Well, a few months ago I was talking to a friend who studies chemistry and she mentioned that her tutor was concerned about falling admissions in their department. This got me thinking about student numbers in engineering. Soon after I noticed an editorial piece in *Science Today* which mentioned that the numbers of postgraduate engineering students had declined in recent years, although the number of female students had increased. I therefore decided to carry out my own research in this field.

3 Read the next question. Underline the key words and think of any synonyms.

> Who was questioned in Dan's survey?
>
> **A**   academic staff in his department
>
> **B**   undergraduate students from other countries
>
> **C**   postgraduate students studying overseas

4 🔊 2.1 Listen and answer the question in 3.

5 Did you hear any distractors? How did you know what the correct answer was? Look at the audio script or listen again and find the distractors.

Matching

6 🔊 2.2 Listen to the final part of the talk. Which statement applies to each of the following people who were interviewed by Dan?

> *Choose **FOUR** answers from the box and write the correct answer, A–F, next to questions 1–4.*
>
> | | |
> |---|---|
> | A | disconnected in the middle of the interview |
> | B | was annoyed by the questions |
> | C | withheld information |
> | D | refused to participate |
> | E | was suspicious of Dan's motives |
> | F | was not easy to locate |
>
> **1**   a postgraduate student from China ....
>
> **2**   a female student at a foreign university ....
>
> **3**   a male undergraduate ....
>
> **4**   a contact of Dan's tutor ....

Unit 6

Speaking skills

1 Which word in each group does NOT collocate with the word in **bold**?

    a a **scientific** *breakthrough/gadget/invention/innovation*

    b *cutting-edge/state-of-the-art/unusual/advanced* **technology**

    c a *recent/scientific/current/groundbreaking* **discovery**

    d a **medical** *breakthrough/discovery/innovation/movement*

    e *pioneering/modern/medical/scientific* **research**

    f a *scientific/new/technological/digital* **revolution**

2 Choose one of the noun phrases in 1 to complete the following Part 2 task card. Use the same noun phrase in each gap.

> Describe (a/an) .... of the last twenty years which you feel has a major influence on your life.
>
> You should say
>
> – what the .... is
>
> – when it started/happened
>
> – what effect it had
>
> and explain how this .... has influenced your life.

3 Spend one minute preparing and making notes. Then practise speaking for two minutes using your notes.

Part 3: Making generalizations

4 Read the following questions about science. Which ones are taken from Speaking Part 1 and which from Part 3?

    1 Which science subject at school do/did you like the most? Why? _____

    2 Do you think life is safer, or more dangerous, with modern technology? _____

    3 Does everybody need to know how to use a computer these days? _____

    4 How has your study of science helped you? _____

    5 Do you think new developments in science often cause more problems than they solve? _____

    6 Which area of scientific research do you think is most important and deserves further research and development? _____

    7 What science subjects do students study at school in your country? _____

    8 Is there anything about science that you dislike? _____

    9 Do you think there are some areas that should be off-limits to scientific research? _____

    10 What effect does new technology have on employment? _____

5 Read two candidates' responses to one of the questions in 1 and answer the questions below.

Candidate A

> Well, I think life is more dangerous as I know many people who have had problems with crime on the Internet. I have a friend who lost some money when she was banking online. Also lots of my friends' parents are worried about them using the Internet because of online bullying and things like that.

Candidate B

> In general, I would say advances in science and technology have made us more secure in many ways. Increased scientific knowledge tends to make us more aware of dangers, and developments in some areas have meant that we are more able to deal with difficulties. Health and medicine would be a good example. Of course, technology is liable to bring dangers too. Take the Internet for instance – that has brought new risks and more criminal activity..

a Which question are they answering? _____

b Which of the candidates provides the best answer? Why? _____

c Underline any words or phrases that Candidate B uses to make generalizations.

d How does Candidate B support these generalizations? _____

6 Read two more candidates' answers to questions in 1. Which question is each one answering? Underline any words or expressions used to make generalizations.

Candidate C

> There are many worthwhile areas of research but, on the whole, I think anything that develops our knowledge and understanding of health and medicine should have further resources and investment. It often seems to be the case that this area is neglected in favour of things like space research and I don't believe that's right.

Candidate D

> As a rule, most jobs would require you to have some skills in this area and I believe in many cases it's probably essential to have a good understanding as you would be expected to use them on a daily basis. Generally speaking, it's more likely to be older generations who haven't got these skills, as they didn't learn them in their younger days and they can have a tendency to be nervous about learning something new.

7 With a partner, ask and answer the Part 3 questions from 1.
Try to make generalizations and support your answers with examples.

Technique

Answers to Part 3 questions should not be too personal, even when you are giving an opinion. You should try to make generalizations, supported by more specific examples. Avoid being too direct with personal opinions or examples from your own life but try to keep your answers more abstract.

Unit 6

Pronunciation

Sounding interested

1 🔊 2.3 Listen to two students responding to this Part 3 question. Which student sounds more interested? Why?

Examiner

> Do you think new developments in science often cause more problems than they solve?

Candidate A

> No, not really. Actually, I would say, that it's the other way round – the problems that science solves far outweigh the problems that it may bring.

Candidate B

> Yes, I think so. Scientific developments often cause lots of problems so sometimes they're not worth it.

Technique

Using flat intonation can show a lack of interest in the topic or examiner and can even make you sound rude. It is important that you use intonation to sound interested and friendly. A change of intonation may occur over a word or phrase or within one word, so that a word may contain a single rise or fall or one word may contain both a rise and a fall.

2 🔊 2.4 Look at two more responses to the same question. Listen and mark where the students' voices rise or fall.

Candidate C

> Absolutely. I mean scientific development can be a positive thing but you need to remember all the negative consequences it can have.

Candidate D

> Well, I suppose it can cause problems, but overall, surely scientific development is a positive thing?

3 Look at this question and the five candidates' responses. Mark where you think their voices will rise or fall.

Examiner

> Do you think there are some areas that should be off-limits to scientific research?

  a Absolutely. I don't think anyone should try to interfere with nature.

  b I'm not sure really. Most research is beneficial but some can be unethical or even dangerous.

  c I really don't think so. Scientists should be free to do what they like.

  d It's a difficult one. If you start prohibiting some research, where do you draw the line?

  e Of course, there should be some sort of guidelines otherwise scientists would do whatever they liked.

  f I agree that there should be some restrictions but it's so difficult to monitor.

4 🔊 2.5 Listen and check whether your ideas were right.

5 Practise saying the sentences aloud paying particular attention to the stress and intonation.

Technique

Don't worry too much about getting the intonation exactly right as intonation can be quite flexible. The important thing to remember is that the voice moves on the stressed words, so think about where the main stresses are in the sentence and move your voice on these.

Exam listening

Section 4

 2.6

Questions 31–34

*Choose the correct letter, **A**, **B**, or **C**.*

31 The number pi

    A   is usually approximated to three decimal points

    B   is an infinite number

    C   can be shown as an exact fraction

32 The date of World Pi Day

    A   is July 22nd

    B   is a fraction shown as a date

    C   is a decimal shown as a date

33 The Ancient Babylonians

    A   discovered an imprecise value of pi

    B   calculated pi as exactly 3

    C   used pi to calculate building size

34 The Ancient Egyptian document mentioned

    A   is the first written record of pi

    B   gives an accurate value of pi

    C   is a reproduction of a previous one

 2.7

Questions 35–40

Which statement applies to each of the following people?

*Choose **SIX** answers from the box and write the correct letter, **A–I**, next to questions 35–40.*

A	had a formula named after him
B	made a mistake
C	proposed a name for the ratio
D	proved the irrationality of pi
E	used a calculator to calculate pi
F	holds the world record for calculating the most digits of pi
G	used shapes to calculate pi
H	achieved a feat of memory
I	proved the transcendence of pi

35 A Greek academic ....

36 A British mathematician ....

37 A German mathematician ....

38 An amateur mathematician ....

39 A French computer programmer ....

40 A postgraduate student ....

7 On the move

UNIT AIMS

LISTENING SKILLS
Summary completion

SPEAKING SKILLS
Part 2: Using a range of language

PRONUNCIATION
Countries and nationalities

EXAM LISTENING
Section 3

Topic talk

1 Look at the picture and answer the questions below.

   a How many different forms of transport can you see?

   b Which form of transport do you most often use on a daily basis?

   c Which form of transport is the most popular in your town/city?

   d Which of these forms of transport has the most benefits?

2 Which form(s) of transport does each speaker (a–h) use? Is the speaker talking about a current benefit or a drawback? Write your answer at the end of each sentence. You will complete the sentences in the next exercise.

   a Parking in the city centre is a nightmare but the local council is planning to introduce a _____ scheme next year.

   _____

   b My city has recently introduced special _____ for us which makes the journey so much quicker as we don't have to worry about cars or pedestrians. _____

   c It can be quite difficult and dangerous as there are no _____ and it's a very busy road. _____

   d Last month I had a _____ on that busy roundabout. I had to call someone out to recover my vehicle.

   _____

   e Car drivers can be so selfish; they always try to _____ and rarely give you enough room – I was knocked off once! _____

   f I find it very frustrating when there's a lot of _____ I can get quite impatient. _____

   g The downside is it can get very crowded during the _____ and it's difficult to get a seat.

   _____

   h It's quick and reliable and because I'm a student I get a _____ fare. _____

i It can be quite dangerous as so many cars speed on the main road; they need to introduce some _____ . _____ .

j That junction is so dangerous – I almost had a _____ with another car last month. _____

3 Complete the sentences in 2 with a word or phrase from the box. Use each word or phrase only once.

> breakdown ■ collision ■ congestion ■ cycle lanes ■ overtake ■ park and ride
> pedestrian crossings ■ rush hour ■ subsidized ■ traffic calming measures

4 Choose the incorrect alternative in each of the questions below.
  a What was the last long _flight/holiday/journey/travel_ you went on?
  b When going long distances, do you prefer to _go/journey/travel_ by train or plane?
  c Would you prefer to go on a package _excursion/tour/holiday_ or travel independently?
  d What is the most famous or popular tourist _destination/attraction/location/centre_ in your country?
  e What are the advantages of travelling _first/upper/business/economy_ class?
  f Do you like holidays with lots of _day trips/expeditions/excursions/sightseeing tours_?
  g When was the last time you took a _long-haul/domestic/short-haul/home/international_ flight?
  h What is your opinion of _eco-/ethical/mass/abroad_ tourism?

5 With a partner, ask and answer the questions in 4.

6 The following words and phrases could all be used to describe tourist destinations. Which ones are positive and which are negative?
  a It's been totally overrun by tourists in recent years and is far too commercialized. _____
  b It's really off the beaten track and you pass some really dramatic scenery to get there. _____
  c It's got a vibrant and cosmopolitan atmosphere. _____
  d There are too many touts and everything is tacky and overpriced.
  _____
  e It's totally unspoilt and there are some breathtaking views.
  _____
  f It's a place of great historical and cultural interest. _____
  g It's a place of real natural beauty and has been largely untouched by tourism. _____
  h It's very remote and isolated and you can feel a little cut off and away from civilization. _____

7 Think of some places you know that could be described in this way. Tell your partner about them.

Listening skills

Summary completion

1 The list below gives seven popular types of overseas voluntary work.
What do you think the work would involve in each case?

  a working with children in an orphanage
  b working on a wildlife conservation project
  c working on a construction project in a rural community
  d working in a rural school
  e working on a rural health education programme
  f working on an environmental conservation project
  g working on a marine conservation project

2 Compare ideas with another student. Then answer the questions below.

  a How easy or difficult do you think each of the jobs would be?
  b Which of the voluntary projects would you choose to work on? Why?
  c In which countries would you be most likely to do one of these projects?
  d At what stage in life might someone volunteer overseas?

> **Exam information**
>
> You will be given a paragraph summarizing part of the listening text. The paragraph will
> not be exactly the same as what you hear, but will include paraphrases and synonyms.
> You should use words from the recording to complete the gaps.

3 The paragraph below is taken from a summary completion task. What is the
general topic? You will complete the gaps in 6.

Complete the summary below.

*Write **NO MORE THAN TWO WORDS AND/OR A NUMBER** for each
answer.*

Dylan recently spent time in South America doing voluntary work and
developing his 1 .... He spent 2 ....
learning Portuguese on an intensive language course. He found the
3 .... was similar to Spanish but he found the accent
difficult. He learnt a lot from his 4 .... He helped at a
5 .... in the Amazon looking after hurt or
6 .... animals before they were returned to the wild.
He then volunteered at a centre for children in the 7 ....
of Rio de Janeiro. The purpose of the centre is to keep the children safe
and away from 8 ....

4 What type of information do you think goes in the gaps (1–8) in 3?
Choose an idea from the box below for each gap.

> a description ■ an aspect of language learning ■ a skill or ability
> a time period ■ a person ■ a place or person ■ a place (x 2)

1 _____

2 _____

3 _____

4 _____

5 _____

6 _____

7 _____

8 _____

5 Look at a candidate's answers to the task. The answers are all incorrect.
Decide what the problem is in each case.

1 Spanish and Portuguese
2 three/six months
3 words
4 his flatmate
5 Peruvian
6 injured
7 project
8 dangerous

6 2.8 Listen and complete the task in 3 by filling in the gaps.

Technique

Note how many words you may use in each gap. Before you listen, underline key words
and phrases in the summary and try to paraphrase them. Try to predict the type of
answers (nouns, verbs, numbers, etc) required for each gap. When you have completed
your answers, make sure that they fit and are grammatically correct.

7 Look at the audio script or
listen again. Find words
and phrases where the
summary has paraphrased
the script.

Speaking skills

Part 2: Using a range of language

1 Think of some countries and tourist attractions in each of the following regions of the world.
   – The Caribbean
   – The Middle East
   – Central America
   – The European Union
   – North Africa
   – Central Asia
   – South-East Asia
   – Scandinavia
   – Australasia
   – North America

2 Which of these parts of the world have you visited? Which would you like to visit most? Why?

3 The list below shows ten reasons why people go on holiday. Which ones are most important to you? Number them 1–10 (1 = least important; 10 = most important).

Why go on holiday?

☐ to visit friends or family

☐ to experience a different country and culture

☐ to spend quality time with my family

☐ to get to know my own country better

☐ to visit places of historical or cultural interest

☐ to relax and unwind

☐ to experience a bit of luxury

☐ to eat good food

☐ to do something active and adventurous

☐ to enjoy the outdoors and nature

4 Compare ideas with a partner. Do you have similar or different tastes in holidays?

5 ◀◻) 2.9 The task cards below are from Speaking Part 2. Listen to a candidate answering one of the questions. Which task is he doing? Make a brief note on the card of the answers he gives to each prompt.

A

Describe a country you would like to visit.

You should say

– where you would like to go

– how you would travel

– what you would do there

and explain why you would like to go to this place.

B

Describe a place you have been to on holiday.

You should say

– where you went

– who you went with

– what you did

and explain what you particularly liked about the holiday.

---

6 Listen again to the first part of the talk and write down words or phrases the speaker uses to avoid repeating the following:

a Malaysia _____

b Kuala Lumpur _____

7 Look at the audio script or listen again and find words and phrases the speaker uses which have similar meanings to:

a cosmopolitan _____

b coast _____

c rainforest _____

d food _____

e tour _____

f wildlife _____

g cheap _____

h difficult _____

i tourists _____

Technique

You will get a higher mark if you use a wide range of vocabulary. Try to avoid repetition of key vocabulary by finding different ways of expressing the same thing.

---

8 Choose one of the tasks from 5 and spend one minute preparing and make notes. Then try to speak for 1–2 minutes on the subject.

Pronunciation

Countries and nationalities

1 ◀)) 2.10 Listen and write the countries you hear in the correct column, according to the word stress.

O	Oo	oO	Ooo	ooO	oOo
Spain	China	Brazil	Italy	Vietnam	Morocco

2 Complete the table by adding nationalities to the correct column. Take care with spelling.

-ish	-(i)an	-ese	-i	other
Spanish	Brazilian	Chinese	Iraqi	French

3 ◀)) 2.11 Listen and mark the stress on the nationality adjectives. Do you notice a pattern?

4 Add more nationalities to the table.

5 Which of the nationality adjectives are also languages? If the adjective is not a language, do you know what language is spoken in that country?

6 The answers to the questions below are all countries or nationalities. Work with a partner and see how many of the answers you know. Pay particular attention to the pronunciation of your answers.

   1 What was the nationality of the scientist and artist Leonardo da Vinci? _____

   2 What language do people in Rio de Janeiro speak? _____

   3 The yen is the currency of which country? _____

   4 What nationality was the artist Pablo Picasso? _____

   5 What nationality were the philosophers Socrates and Aristotle? _____

   6 What language do people in Tokyo speak? _____

   7 What nationality was the composer Tchaikovsky? _____

   8 Baghdad is the capital city of which country? _____

   9 Which language do people in Oslo speak? _____

  10 What language do people in Paris speak? _____

  11 What is the biggest country in the world? _____

  12 In which country would you find the cities of Berlin and Munich? _____

7 Make up some more questions to test another pair.

Exam listening

Section 3

 2.12

Questions 21–24

*Choose the correct letter, **A**, **B** or **C**.*

21 The number of vehicles on the road

    A is around 100 billion

    B is doubling every year

    C will have doubled in twenty years

22 Where has a payment been introduced to restrict city traffic?

    A some cities in China

    B London

    C Moscow

23 Which cause of traffic congestion is NOT given?

    A it can be caused by the action of a single driver

    B it can be caused by bad driving

    C it can be caused by unexpected events on the road

24 Congestion waves affect

    A any junction where traffic merges

    B motorways only

    C all roads in cities

 2.13

Questions 25–30

Complete the summary below.

*Write **NO MORE THAN TWO WORDS OR A NUMBER** for each answer.*

A system was developed to control traffic congestion on the M25 motorway. Experts use
25 .... information from the motorway to set **26** .... according
to traffic build-up. However, in order to maintain a steady flow of traffic, the number of
vehicles on the roads should not exceed **27** .... per lane per hour, which is far
fewer than the number on **28** .... of the motorway. One solution could be to
fit the car with **29** .... and a computer. The system would be activated when
approaching an area of congestion and the computer would then regulate the acceleration
and **30** .... to help the car to pass easily through the congestion.

8 Friends and family

UNIT AIMS

LISTENING SKILLS
Listening to numbers and letters
Form completion

SPEAKING SKILLS
Part 3: Avoiding repetition using substitution and ellipsis

PRONUNCIATION
Strong and weak forms

EXAM LISTENING
Section 1

Topic talk

1 Look at the pictures and answer the questions below.

   a Which picture most closely resembles the family you grew up in?
   b Is there any such thing as a typical family nowadays?
   c Do you think the family unit has changed over the years? In what way?

2 Match the sentences (1–10) with their extensions (a–i). Use the key words in bold to help you.

   1 My next-door neighbours, Paul and Sophie, are a **married couple** with two young children; _____
   2 It's important for young people to have appropriate **role models**; _____
   3 Some parents can be **over-protective**; _____
   4 The **average family size** is becoming smaller; _____
   5 My parents weren't very **strict** with me when I was young; _____
   6 Most brothers and sisters experience some degree of **jealousy** and **competition**; _____
   7 **Childcare** can be very expensive; _____
   8 My friend Sally was raised by **foster parents** who later **adopted** her; _____
   9 After he was **widowed**, Phil brought up his daughters on his own; _____
   10 I **grew up** in a house with my parents, grandparents and an aunt uncle and cousins; _____

   a we were a traditional **extended family**.
   b this means returning to work after **childbirth** can be difficult for some mothers.
   c this **sibling rivalry** can result in small fights and arguments.
   d luckily he had support from other **single-parent** families.
   e they are a typical **nuclear family**.
   f then they have people they can look up to and learn from, who will have a **positive influence** on their lives.
   g her own mother was unable to **look after** her.
   h they do not allow their children to take risks and become **independent**.
   i the **birth rate** in many countries has decreased recently.
   j in fact they were very **lenient** and rarely **punished** me.

3 Compare the following situations, thinking of advantages and disadvantages.

   a living in a nuclear family vs. living in an extended family
   b growing up with strict or over-protective parents vs. lenient parents
   c a falling birth rate vs. a rising birth rate

4 Complete the phrasal verbs with an appropriate preposition or adverb from the box. Some of the words may be used more than once.

> after ■ apart ■ away ■ back ■ back on ■ down
> on ■ out ■ over ■ up ■ up with ■ up to

a My older brother always did really well at school and as I was growing _____ I found it very hard to live _____ his reputation.

b Claire and I go _____ years – we first met at primary school and have been friends every since. We have many happy memories to look _____ .

c I don't take _____ either of my parents – we are very different. Maybe that's why we get _____ so well!

d Kris and Annabelle have finally decided to settle _____ and get married – I hope it works _____ for them.

e My grandfather passed _____ in January – I don't think he ever really got _____ the death of my grandmother last year.

f When I was very young I really looked _____ my older sister – I thought she was fantastic! But as we got older we grew _____ and now I don't often see her very often.

g We have brought _____ our children to be polite and respectful so I find it difficult to put _____ bad behaviour from others..

5 Choose the adjective which is the opposite of the other three.

a creative/dull/resourceful/talented

b changeable/faithful/loyal/reliable _____

c charitable/generous/helpful/selfish _____

d amusing/funny/witty/serious/ _____

e cheerful/cynical/optimistic/positive _____

f ambitious/determined/lazy/motivated _____

g friendly/good company/outgoing/reserved/ _____

h aggressive/calm/laid-back/relaxed _____

6 In Speaking Part 2 you may be asked to describe a person. Complete the sentences below using an example from your friends, family or someone else you know.

a The family member I take after most is …

b A friend who goes back years is …

c Someone I look up to is …

d Someone I look back on with fond memories is …

e A family member I get on really well with is …

7 With a partner, describe the people in 6 using some of the adjectives in 5. Develop your ideas with reasons and examples.

Example
The family member I take after most is my grandfather. We are both quite sociable and enjoy meeting people and chatting. And we're both very cheerful and optimistic – we always try to look on the bright side. Something that is different about us is our sense of humour - he's very funny and loves telling jokes and making people laugh – I can't do that.

Listening skills

Listening to numbers and letters

> ### Exam information
> Questions which include listening for numbers and spelling may occur in any part of the Listening test, particularly Section 1.

> ### Technique
> Take care with easily confused numbers and letters like *e* and *i*, *g* and *j*, *13* and *30*.

1 🔊 2.14 Listen to the following and choose the correct answer.

1 The reference number is
   A GE435HAX
   B JE435HIX
   C GI435AIH

2 The address is
   A 14 Wainwright Road
   B 40 Wainright Road
   C 40 Wainwright Road

3 The postcode is
   A CV13 6JG
   B CB30 6GJ
   C CV30 6JG

4 The Flight number is
   A EX 6538
   B EH 6358
   C EA 6358

5 The credit card number is
   A 6595 4450 5869 5899
   B 6595 4430 5869 5855
   C 6595 4420 8569 5855

6 His surname is
   A Lindsay
   B Lindsey
   C Lyndsey

7 Her passport number is
   A 925465006
   B 935465006
   C 935463006

8 The telephone number is
   A 07448396483
   B 07448356483
   C 07448369483

9 The email address is
   A williams14@mail.com
   B william40@mail.com
   C william14@mail.com

10 The room number is
   A B583
   B V983
   C B938

Form completion

2 Look at the form below. Predict the type of information that will appear in each gap.

3 2.15 Listen to part of a telephone conversation and complete the form below. Use no more than THREE WORDS AND/OR A NUMBER in each space.

> ### Technique
> The word or number you need might not necessarily be the one you hear first as the speaker may correct himself/herself. Listen carefully to make sure you write down the corrected version.

⊙ ⊙ ⊙ ▭

Abbey Car Hire

Booking Form

Car size	medium family car
Name	Steven **1** ....
Address	3 Hamilton House, **2** .... , Stretton
Postcode	ST17 5BU
Telephone	**3** ....
Pick up	**4** .... 25 April at **5** ....
Drop off	**6** .... at **7** ....
Total charge	£87.50 (including insurance)
Driving Licence	**8** ....
Extras	**9** .... (£10)
Reference	**10** ....

Unit 8

Speaking skills

Part 3: Avoiding repetition using substitution and ellipsis

1 Read the two responses to the examiner's question. Which response is better? Why?

Examiner

> Do you think it's important for friends to have similar personalities?

Candidate A

> No I don't think it's important for friends to have similar personalities. It would be very boring and predictable if friends all had the same personality. I think sometimes the most interesting relationships are the relationships between very different personalities. People sometimes assume that relationships between different personalities can lead to arguments but they don't have to lead to arguments. For example, one person could be quite sociable whilst the person's friend isn't sociable, but together the two friends' personalities can make a good balance.

Candidate B

> No I don't think so. It would be very boring and predictable if friends all had the same character. I think sometimes the most interesting relationships are the ones between very different individuals. People sometimes assume that this type of friendship can lead to arguments but they don't have to. For example, one person could be quite sociable whilst her friend isn't, but together their personalities can make a good balance.

2 Underline the parts of Candidate B's answer which are used to avoid repetition. Which parts of Candidate A's answer are they replacing?

3 Match the words and phrases you identified in 2 with the techniques to avoid repetition below.

Reference: using a pronoun (*he, it, their, this, these*) to refer to something already mentioned: _____

_____

Lexical cohesion: replacing one item of vocabulary with another which has a similar meaning: _____

_____

Substitution: replacing one item with a pronoun or other item (an auxiliary verb, *so, one(s), neither, not*): _____

_____

Ellipsis: omitting a word or phrase completely: _____

_____

4 Match the statements (1–8) with an appropriate extension (a–h).

1 One of the main duties of parents is to provide their children with a loving and secure environment. _____

2 Being shy and reserved has not affected his ability to be successful in life. _____

3 The number of older people in society has increased significantly in recent years. _____

4 Growing up bilingual can bring many career and educational advantages for children, _____

5 You should try to have a positive and optimistic outlook on life. _____

6 Watching too much television can have serious consequences for young children. _____

7 Some people think that it is important to give money to help poor people overseas, _____

8 My grandparents had a great influence on me as I was growing up, _____

a This rise has led to a need for better healthcare provision for the elderly.

b Another one is to bring them up with a good sense of what is right and wrong and to give them as good an education as possible.

c but it can also lead to confusion and divided loyalties if their parents do not speak the same language as their friends and other outsiders.

d and continue to do so now, even though they are both in their eighties.

e Neither has his lack of formal education or qualifications.

f These can include poor concentration and aggressive or antisocial behaviour which may affect their education.

g Doing so can allow you to take control of your life and reduce stress.

h but I believe such a view is unjustified when people are suffering hardship closer to home.

5 For each of the paired sentences in 4, underline any examples of reference, lexical cohesion, substitution and ellipsis.

6 Cross out any unnecessary words in the following questions.

a Do parents read to their children as much as they should read to their children?

b Should couples who have children be given more financial benefits than couples who don't have children?

c Do you think that couples who share the housework equally are likely to have fewer arguments than couples who don't share the housework equally?

d Do you help around the house as much as you could help around the house?

e Do young children who go to nursery have more opportunities for social interaction than children who don't go to nursery?

f Do you think men tend to help more around the home than they used to help around the home?

7 With a partner, ask and answer the questions in 6.

Pronunciation

Strong and weak forms

1 Complete the following statements with a phrase from the box.

> it is ■ I was ■ I would ■ I wouldn't ■ my friends are
> others haven't ■ to do so ■ would like to

   a Some teenagers in my school are not very well-behaved but fortunately

      all _____ .

   b I've had a very happy childhood so I sometimes forget that _____ .

   c Spending quality time together is important for most families but

      unfortunately it's not always possible _____ .

   d Some people think that having a child is not a major responsibility but

      obviously _____ .

   e My parents didn't have a good education so they were determined that

      _____ .

   f Not everyone wants to keep in touch with their old school friends when they

      leave school but I _____ .

   g I would like to bring up my children in a large family just as

      _____ .

   h Many of my friends say they want to leave home to study overseas but

      _____ .

2 ◀) 2.16 Listen to the sentences. Are the phrases that you added in 1, strong or weak?

3 Practise saying the statements aloud, paying particular attention to the stress.

4 Look at the sentences (a–h) below. Are the underlined words strong or weak?

   a I'd like <u>to</u> leave home one day but I'm not sure if I'm ready <u>to</u> yet.
   b I'm lucky – I'<u>ve</u> had far better opportunities in life than my parents <u>did</u>.
   c I thought young children <u>could</u> be difficult but teenagers <u>can</u> too!
   d Couples who <u>don't</u> have much money often wait until they <u>do</u> before having children.
   e I loved being part of a big family when I <u>was</u> young and I still <u>do</u>.
   f Being shy <u>has</u> never <u>been</u> a disadvantage <u>for</u> me, but I know it <u>can be for</u> some.
   g When I <u>was</u> young I would <u>have</u> loved <u>to</u> have an older brother <u>to</u> look up <u>to</u>.
   h Children today <u>are</u> sometimes more confident about using technology than their parents and teachers <u>are</u>.

5 ◀) 2.17 Listen to check. Then practise saying the sentences, paying particular attention to the strong and weak forms.

Exam listening

Section 1

 2.18

Questions 1–3

*Choose the correct letter **A**, **B**, or **C**.*

1   The festival is held

   A   every year

   B   twice a year

   C   once every two years

2   The programme contains

   A   one or two events suitable for children

   B   many different events for children

   C   not enough events for children

3   The leaflet advises people

   A   to reserve tickets for popular events

   B   to buy tickets on the day

   C   to buy one ticket for all events

2.19

Questions 4–10

Complete the notes below.

*Write **NO MORE THAN TWO WORDS AND/OR A NUMBER** for each answer.*

EASTFIELD FAMILY ARTS FESTIVAL
BOOKING FORM
NAME: Alan Hardy
EMAIL: **4** .... @mailgroup.com
TELEPHONE: **5** ....
TICKETS WILL BE EMAILED **6** .... PRIOR TO EVENT

Date	Event	Number of tickets required	Price per ticket
Friday July 4	The Stags traditional and modern **7** .... music	2 adults 2 children	£8.50
Saturday July 5	Robin Hood Eastfield **8**	**9** .... 2 children	£5
	Gordon Hayburn Singer songwriter	1 adult	£7.50
Sunday July 6	Crash Irish drumming group	1 adults 2 children	**10** ....

9 Spend spend spend!

UNIT AIMS

LISTENING SKILLS
Labelling a diagram
Identifying the speaker's attitude

SPEAKING SKILLS
Part 2: Describing objects
Follow-up questions

PRONUNCIATION
Word stress in nouns and verbs

EXAM LISTENING
Section 3

Topic talk

1 Read the sayings about money (a–d) and answer the questions.

  a *Money is a good servant but a bad master.*
  b *Money doesn't grow on trees.*
  c *A fool and his money are soon parted.*
  d *The best things in life are free.*
  1 What do you understand by each saying?
  2 Do you have a similar saying in your language?
  3 Do you agree with the sentiment expressed in each saying? Why/Why not?

2 Choose the correct alternative in italics to complete the questions.

  1 What is your biggest *expense/cost* each month?
  2 Do you regularly pay into a *deposit/payment* account?
  3 Would you prefer to *be in debit/be in debt* to a bank or to a family member?
  4 What's the best way to *owe/save* money for the future?
  5 Do credit cards encourage people to buy things that they can't really *pay for/spend*?
  6 Should children have to earn their *pocket money/savings*?
  7 Have you ever *won/been left* money when someone died?
  8 How important to you is having a large *expenditure/income*?
  9 What's the best way to *cut back/save up* on household spending?
  10 Which is more important for governments to focus on – health or education *expenses/expenditure*?

3 Replace the words you chose in 2 with one of the words below, which has the same or a similar meaning.

> afford ■ allowance ■ economize ■ outgoing ■ inherited ■ invest
> owe ■ salary ■ savings ■ spending

4 Match the responses (a–j) with the questions in 2.

a Overreliance on credit facilities can lead to debt and even bankruptcy.

b Public spending in both these areas is a priority. _____

c For most people it's their accommodation but I'm lucky – I live with my parents so I don't have a mortgage and I don't have to pay rent.

_____

d Probably by cutting down on the amount you spend on

non-essential items and luxuries. _____

e Doing small jobs around the house should teach them the value of

money. _____

f I'm happy as long as my earnings exceed my outgoings – I don't mind

not being well-off. _____

g I used to, but inflation has been so high recently I can only just

manage to get by on what I earn. _____

h Banks are more likely to charge you high interest rates.

i I was lucky to come into some money from my aunt at

a time when I was very hard up. _____

j Investments in stocks and shares can be risky if the market falls.

_____

5 With a partner, ask and answer the questions in 2. Remember to give reasons for your answers.

6 How often do you use the following types of retailers? What type of goods do you buy from them?
What are the advantages and disadvantages of each?

a national chain stores or supermarkets
b independent local shops
c large online retailers
d second-hand or charity shops
e online auction sites

7 Decide which adjective in italics is the opposite of the other two.

a It's not a good idea to spend a lot of money on online auction sites as the goods may turn out to be *worthless/priceless/of no value*.
b If you're *hard up/well off/badly off* you shouldn't spend money on entertainment or holidays.
c Buying in bulk can be a more *economical/cost-effective/costly* way to shop for non-perishable groceries.
d It's a good idea to support small local shops but unfortunately, they can be quite *discounted/overpriced/costly*.
e One of the best ways to be *thrifty/extravagant/economical* is to buy second-hand goods.
f *Made-to-measure/off-the-shelf/custom-made* goods are always of superior quality.
g Buying *designer/mass-produced/off-the-peg* clothes does not allow for individuality.

8 Do you agree or disagree with the statements in 7? Tell your partner, giving reasons and examples.

Listening skills

Labelling a diagram

1 Look at the different ways of paying for things and answer the questions.
- cash (coins and notes)
- bank transfer
- cheque
- credit card
- debit card
- online payment system

a Which one(s) do you use most often on a daily basis?
b How much cash do you usually carry on you?
c Which method of payment do you think is the safest?

Exam information

In label completion tasks, you will be given a diagram, chart or plan with labels to complete. You will be given a specified number of words to use for each gap. The questions will be numbered in the same order as you hear them.

Technique

Some of the labels may already be complete so you can use these as a reference. The words in the partially completed labels may include paraphrases of what you will hear or key words to listen out for. Before you listen, use the diagram to predict the answers.

2 Look at the diagrams and answer the questions.

a What do the diagrams show? _____

b How could you describe the appearance? _____

c What do the labels indicate? Try to predict the answers. _____

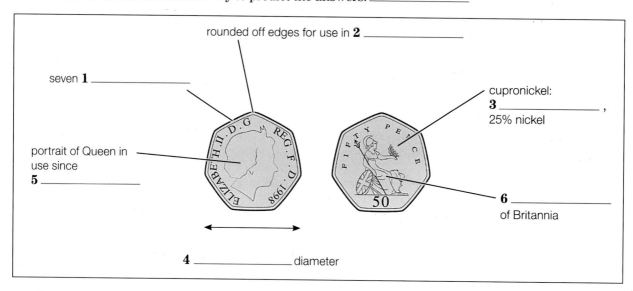

rounded off edges for use in **2** _____

seven **1** _____

portrait of Queen in use since **5** _____

cupronickel: **3** _____ , 25% nickel

6 _____ of Britannia

4 _____ diameter

3 2.20 Listen and complete the labels (1–6) using NO MORE THAN TWO WORDS OR A NUMBER IN EACH SPACE.

Identifying the speaker's attitude

4 🔊 2.21 Listen to five short dialogues in which two speakers, A and B, respond to statements. In each case, decide which speaker agrees with the statement and which speaker disagrees.

5 Listen again to the speakers in 4 and complete the expressions they use to agree and disagree.

Agreement

It's certainly _____ .

_____ they_____ !

I _____ agree with you _____ .

Well, you have _____ .

Oh, _____ !

Disagreement

_____ they can't!

Surely that's a _____ ?

I'm not sure that's a _____ .

It's never been _____ .

You're _____ .

6 🔊 2.22 Listen to a conversation between Anne and Paul. Which opinion does each person express? Write *A* (Anne), *P* (Paul) or *B* (both) beside each opinion (1–6).

a The amount of student debt is not surprising. _____

b Students don't have enough time to work alongside their studies.

_____

c Student jobs are badly paid. _____

d Students would prefer not to have to depend on their families.

_____

e It's better to get a job rather than go to university. _____

f It's difficult for graduates to find work.

Technique

Some questions require you to identify the speaker's attitude or opinion. Sometimes this can be through the language he/she uses but the expression and tone of voice will also give you important clues.

Speaking skills

Part 2: Describing objects

1 Read the three short texts in which someone talks about a possession. Match each description to one of the items in the box below.

> an item of clothing ■ a valuable antique ■ an item of technology
> a piece of furniture ■ a picture ■ a vehicle ■ a piece of jewellery

A It was something I had wanted for such a long time. I ordered it online but I had to wait a while for it to be delivered. I was so excited when it actually arrived. My friends were all very jealous as it's the latest model and I was the first to get it. It's incredible that something so tiny has so many different features; it's much better than my old one and can do so many things. I really like the design – it's very slim and streamlined. I wasn't sure which colour to choose but in the end I went for the silver option, which I'm really pleased with. I use it all the time and I couldn't live without it.

_____

B It's of great sentimental value as it used to be my great-grandmother's so you could say it's a family heirloom. She was given it for her 21st birthday so it really is quite ancient now. It's not in perfect condition as the gold has a few scratches on it but I think that gives it character. I don't often wear it and I usually keep it locked away but I do put it on for special family occasions It always makes my father very happy to see it on my finger. It means a great deal to me and I hope to pass it down to my children or grandchildren.

_____

C I spotted it in an old junk shop and it immediately appealed to me as it looks as if it's got an interesting history. I love all the little marks on the wood and the hand-painted drawer knobs are really beautiful. I don't think it's very valuable but I'm really fond of it and I have it on display in my living room. Visitors often admire it and ask me about it. They think that I bought it in some exotic faraway country – they're always surprised when I tell them I paid £5 for it in an old second-hand shop. It's not just decorative though – it's useful too and is great for storage. I keep all my DVDs in it.

_____

2 Read the descriptions again. Complete the table below with notes for each point.

	A	B	C
General description	_the latest model_		
Where they got it	_online_		
Appearance			
What it's used for			
What it means to the speaker			

3 Choose a possession that is important to you and make notes in the table below.

Possession	
Where you got it	
General description	
Appearance	
What it's used for	
What it means to you	

4 Practise speaking for two minutes using your notes.

5 The task card below is taken from Speaking Part 2. How is this task different from the one you have just done?

> Describe something you saved up for.
> You should say
> – what it is
> – where you bought it
> – how long you had to save for it
> and explain why you wanted to buy it.

6 Take one minute to think and make notes. Then practise speaking for two minutes using your notes.

Follow-up questions

7 Look at these possible follow-up questions to Part 2 tasks. Match the student responses (a-d) to each of the questions.

Exam information

Part 2 of the Speaking test will usually be followed by one or two follow-up questions, related to the topic you have just talked about. These questions are designed to conclude this part of the test and lead into the two-way discussion in Part 3.

1 How do you plan to use this object in the future? _____

2 Was it easy to save money for this? _____

3 Are there any other ways to buy things other than saving money? _____

4 Do you prefer to spend or save money? _____

Technique

You are not expected to give particularly long answers to the follow-up questions. The questions may give you an idea of how the discussion in Part 3 is going to continue.

a I absolutely love shopping, particularly for clothes and music so that's where most of my money goes, I'm afraid.

b If you haven't got the money you might buy things on credit or take out a loan for an expensive item.

c I still use it every day and I expect that will continue, at least until I replace it with the next model.

d I suppose I was motivated to do it quickly so that helped but it still took me a long time to get enough together to afford it.

8 With a partner, ask and answer the questions, relating them to the answer you gave in 6.

Pronunciation

Word stress in nouns and verbs

1 Are the underlined words in the following sentences nouns or verbs?

  a If the goods are faulty we will give a full <u>refund</u>.
  b I like shopping for fresh <u>produce</u> in local farmers' markets.
  b I don't like giving money as a <u>present</u> – it doesn't seem very personal.
  d Interest rates are set to <u>increase</u> again next month.
  e I took it back to the shop but they wouldn't <u>refund</u> the money.
  f I wasn't sure when to <u>present</u> him with the bill for my work.
  g I don't know how that shop manages to <u>produce</u> such inexpensive clothing.
  h The recent <u>increase</u> in the cost of living has made life very difficult for many families.

2 🔊 2.23 Listen to the sentences, paying particular attention to the word stress of the underlined words. Write the sentence (a, b, etc) next to the stress patterns below. Do you notice a pattern?

  Oo _____

  oO _____

3 Practise saying the sentences aloud, paying particular attention to the word stress of the underlined verbs and nouns.

4 Decide if the underlined words in the following questions are verbs or nouns.

  a If you bought something which had a <u>defect</u>, would you take it back and ask for a <u>refund</u>?
  b Has there been an <u>increase</u> in the cost of public <u>transport</u> in your town recently?
  c Would you <u>object</u> to paying higher taxes if public services were <u>increased</u>?
  d Do you prefer to buy fresh <u>produce</u> locally or fruit and vegetables <u>imported</u> from other countries?
  e Do you always take a <u>present</u> when you are <u>invited</u> to someone's house?
  f Would you <u>refuse</u> to work if your employer tried to change your <u>contract</u> or working conditions?
  g Should the public be <u>permitted</u> to read a company's financial <u>records</u> or should they be kept private?
  h Do you think that students have a right to <u>protest</u> about <u>increases</u> in fees?

5 Mark the word stress for each of the underlined words.

6 🔊 2.24 Listen and check. Practise saying the questions.

7 With a partner, ask and answer the questions in 4.

Technique

The unstressed vowels may become very weak and the sound may change. Notice the difference between the noun /ˈprɒdjuːs/ and the verb /prəˈdjuːs/.

Exam listening

Section 3

 2.25

Questions 21–24.

*Choose the correct letter, **A**, **B** or **C**.*

21 Rob believes that

    A   career success always brings financial gain.

    B   not all successful people are well paid.

    C   people in low-paid jobs are not successful.

22 According to Isabelle you should judge someone's success by

    A   their contribution to society.

    B   how much pay they get.

    C   how much unpaid work they do.

23 Isabelle thinks that famous successful people

    A   are not always talented.

    B   earn too much money.

    C   do not deserve their wealth.

24 According to Rob, why do people undertake academic study?

    A   because they want a well-paid career.

    B   because they love their subject.

    C   because they don't know what to do.

 2.26

Questions 25–30

*Label the bar chart. Write **NO MORE THAN THREE WORDS OR A NUMBER** for each answer.*

Most important indicators of success (%)

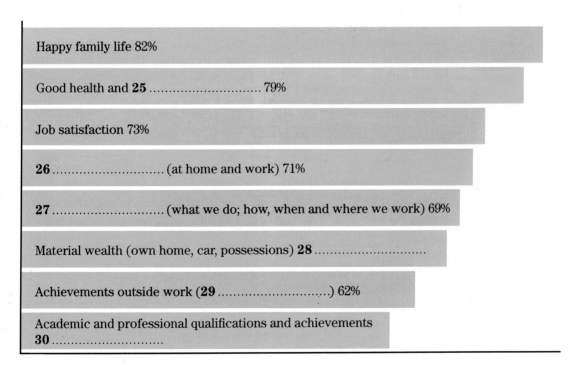

Happy family life 82%

Good health and **25** 79%

Job satisfaction 73%

26 .... (at home and work) 71%

27 .... (what we do; how, when and where we work) 69%

Material wealth (own home, car, possessions) **28** ....

Achievements outside work (**29** ....) 62%

Academic and professional qualifications and achievements **30** ....

10 Time

UNIT AIMS

LISTENING SKILLS
Understanding structure and flow
Flowchart completion

SPEAKING SKILLS
Part 3: Speculating and speaking
hypothetically

PRONUNCIATION
Stress in compound adjectives

EXAM LISTENING
Section 4

Topic talk

1 Look at the pictures and answer the questions below.

   a What is your favourite time of day? And your least favourite? Why?

   b At which time of day do you function most efficiently?

   c In which situations do you feel time moves too fast or too slowly?

2 Complete the statements with a verb from the box to make time collocations.

> allow ■ devote ■ find ■ have ■ reduce ■ save ■ spend ■ waste

   a I _____ a lot of my free time watching TV.

   b I _____ myself plenty of time to get ready in the morning.

   c I'd like to _____ the amount of time I spend sleeping.

   d I wish I could _____ more time to doing voluntary work.

   e I often _____ a lot of time chatting to friends online.

   f I never seem to be able to _____ the time to help my mum
around the house.

   g I'd like to learn a musical instrument, but I don't _____ time.

   h I could _____ time if I organized my work better.

3 Make the statements true for you. Tell your partner.

4 In the following sentences, which adjective is NOT possible?

  a Preserving historical sites for *subsequent/coming/preceding* generations is not a priority in today's world.

  b Unless measures are taken to protect them, *age-old/antique/ancient* traditions will eventually die out.

  c There is no point in analysing events of *bygone/old/ancient* times – they have no relevance today.

  d *Modern/Present/Contemporary* society is far too concerned with material wealth and consumerism.

  e *Emerging/Rising/Existing* technologies are unlikely to make a difference to the world's energy problems.

  f A country's *traditional/ancient/elderly* customs only survive today because of global tourism.

  g *Modern/Contemporary/New* history can teach us far more than *old/ancient/early history*.

5 Do you agree or disagree with the statements in 4? Give reasons and examples for your answers.

6 In different sections of the Speaking test you will be expected to talk about the past, present and future, using a range of language and structures. Do the statements below refer to past, present or future or more than one time?

  a Until <u>recently</u> we'd go to the seaside every summer holiday. _____

  b The recent changes are <u>bound</u> to make a difference <u>before long</u>. _____

  c We <u>tend</u> to take mobile phones for granted <u>in this day and age</u>. _____

  d I don't <u>make a habit</u> of being late but I'm just about to miss the flight – it leaves in 15 minutes and I'm stuck in traffic. _____

  e <u>Rarely</u> have I been so excited about something. _____

  f I've been learning English <u>for years</u>. _____

  g A big increase in population is <u>predicted</u> <u>over the coming decade</u>. _____

  h I <u>can't see</u> this happening in the <u>short term</u>. _____

  i I've been applying for jobs recently and I <u>aim</u> to have one <u>by the time</u> I finish my degree.

7 Replace each of the underlined words or expressions in 6 with a word or expression from the box with a similar meaning.

> are inclined ■ a short time ago ■ don't anticipate ■ forecast ■ in the next ten years
> near future ■ nowadays ■ plan ■ practise ■ seldom ■ sure
> since I started school ■ sooner or later ■ used to ■ when

8 Make notes on each of the following using your own ideas and experiences.
  a something you used to enjoy doing when you were young
  b something that is predicted to happen in the next few years
  c something you plan to do in the near future
  d something you've been doing for a long time
  e something which is bound to happen before long
  f something which you make a habit of doing

9 With a partner, describe your ideas and experiences in 8. Remember to develop your ideas with reasons and examples.

Listening skills

Understanding structure and flow

1 With a partner, ask and answer the questions below.

   a Do you think time management is important? Why/Why not?

   b How well do you manage your time?

   c Have you ever been in a situation where you were late for an important event or deadline? How did you feel?

2 🔊 2.27 The sentences below come from the first part of a talk about time management. Put the sentences in a logical order. Then listen to check your answers.

   a <u>Then</u> we'll consider the implications of poor time management in a little more detail by considering a specific case study. _____

   b So <u>turning now to</u> the first part of my talk – poor time management. _____

   c <u>Let me begin by</u> outlining the main areas of my talk today. _____

   d So <u>as I was saying</u>, there will be a chance at the end of my talk for any questions you might have. _____

   e <u>By the way</u>, there are leaflets being passed round with details of these strategies – please take a copy away with you. _____

   f <u>Firstly</u>, I'll briefly discuss how poor time management can affect us in the workplace and at home. _____

   g <u>Finally</u>, we'll look at some simple techniques that I hope will help you organize your time more effectively, before question time. _____

   h <u>In addition</u>, I have a number of information packs and posters which you are welcome to take if you're interested. _____

> ### Technique
> Linking words and phrases are used to organize talks and lectures. Listening out for these will help you follow the flow and structure of the talk.

3 What is the function of each of the underlined phrases in 2? Add them to the table below. Which function does not have an example?

Starting	
Adding	
Sequencing	
Changing topic	
Digressing (going off the topic)	
Returning to the topic	
Concluding	

4 Add words and phrases from the box below to the table in 3.

> after that ■ to conclude ■ furthermore ■ having talked about X, let's now ... ■ I'll start by incidentally ■ lastly ■ let's now consider ■ moving on to ■ next ■ returning to my main point secondly ■ to sum up

Flowchart completion

5 Look at the notes and flowchart below and answer the questions.

   a What do they describe?

   b What type of information is missing in each gap?

   c How does the information in each stage of the flow chart relate to other stages? Describe the process to your partner.

6 2.28 Listen to the first section and complete the notes below using NO MORE THAN TWO WORDS for each question.

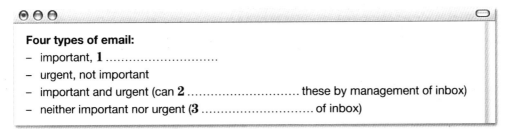

Four types of email:

– important, **1** ....

– urgent, not important

– important and urgent (can **2** .... these by management of inbox)

– neither important nor urgent (**3** .... of inbox)

7 2.29 Listen to the first section and complete the notes below using Listen to the next part and complete the notes in the flow chart with NO MORE THAN THREE WORDS in each answer.

Technique

Spend time examining the flowchart and deciding how each stage relates to the ones around it. You will hear the questions in the same order as they appear on the flowchart. Listen carefully for 'signpost' words and phrases that will help you identify the structure and flow.

New email arrives in inbox

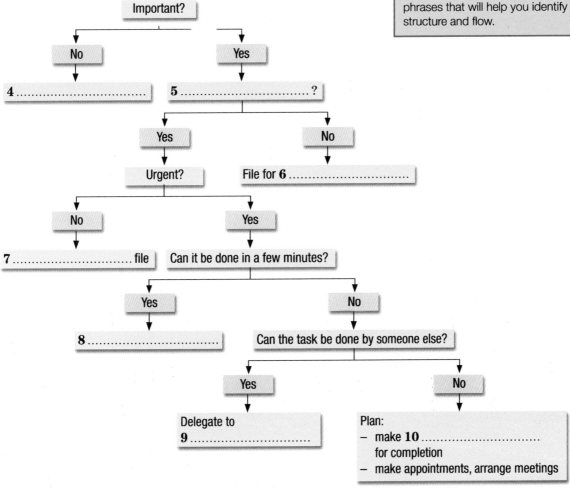

Speaking skills

Part 3: Speculating and speaking hypothetically

> **Exam information**
>
> In Part 3 of the Speaking test you will be expected to speak hypothetically about the past, present or future and speculate about the future.

1 The following Part 3 questions all require you to speak hypothetically or speculate about the future. Decide what the general topic is in each case.

   a How do you think the tourist industry will develop in the future? _____

   b How may eating habits change in the next few years? _____

   c To what extent do you think advertising affects the way people shop? _____

   d Do you think it is important for young people to have role models? _____

   e How can sport bring people from different countries closer together? _____

   f What effect can watching television have on children? _____

   g How do you think the leisure industry will develop in the coming years? _____

   h Do you think people should stay in the same jobs all their lives? _____

   i How would you feel if you had the chance to travel in space? _____

   j What will the situation be if the use of private cars continues to increase? _____

2 ◀))2.30–2.33 Listen to candidates answering four of the questions in 1. Which questions do they answer?

3 Listen again and complete these sentences from the students' answers. Then check your answers in the audio script on pages 116–7.

   a ... most employers _____ it if their workers _____ broad experience in different work contexts.

   b Personally, if I _____ the opportunity, I _____ to get as much different experience as possible.

   c There _____ not the slightest chance of promotion if you _____ this experience ...

   d ... if that _____ , there _____ a greater emphasis on healthy fast food ...

   e ... if we _____ a great park and ride scheme in the city, it _____ even worse.

   f It _____ any better _____ serious measures are taken..

   g The trouble is, _____ you provide better and cheaper public transport, people _____ the convenience of using a private car.

   h It's quite possible that there are products I _____ if I _____ an advert for them.

4 Complete the table below with the sentences in 3, according to the time reference and degree of possibility. The first one has been done as an example.

	Past	Present/Future
Possible		
Hypothetical		

5 Look at the audio script on pages 116–7. The words and phrases in **bold** all speculate about the future. Add them to the table below, according to the degree of certainty or probability.

Certain	Probable	Possible	Improbable	Impossible

6 Complete these sentences about the other questions in 1 using your own ideas.

1 How do you think the tourist industry will develop in the future?

It's highly likely that the tourist industry will _____

I doubt whether _____

2 Do you think it is important for young people to have role models?

Unless children have _____

There's a good likelihood that _____

3 How can sport bring people from different countries closer together?

International sporting events are likely to _____

If sportsmen and women _____

4 What effect can watching television have on children?

If children _____

They are bound to _____

5 How do you think the leisure industry will develop in the coming years?

It's quite possible that _____

It's unlikely that _____

6 How would you feel if you had the chance to travel in space?

There's not much chance of _____

If I had _____

7 With a partner, use the language of speculation and hypothesis to discuss the following.

a plans for your future studies or career
b the development of your hometown in the future
c the effects of the Internet on young people
d current and future population growth
e the benefits and drawbacks of international aid organizations
f recent and future developments in medicine

Pronunciation

Stress in compound adjectives

1 Underline the compound adjective in the following pairs of sentences. Where do you think the stress falls?

   a Her books on time travel have been best-selling.

   b She's written a number of best-selling books on time travel.

   c The effects of postponing the election will be far-reaching.

   d The postponement of the election will have far-reaching effects.

2 🔊 2.34 Listen to check your answers.

3 Where does the stress fall if the adjective is followed by a noun? Where does it fall if the adjective is used without a noun?

Technique

The stress in compound adjectives is generally on the second word of the adjective. However, before a noun, the stress will generally shift to the first word, eg *The clothes in the shop are mass-pro<u>duced</u>. It's a <u>mass</u>-produced dress.*

---

4 Underline the stressed syllable in the compound adjectives in the following questions.

   a What are the benefits and drawbacks of buying mass-produced goods? What about products that are custom-made?

   b What are some of the long-term effects of flooding?

   c What is the most cost-effective way to travel in your country?

   d How can cross-cultural understanding be best achieved?

   e What's the best way of keeping up-to-date with world news?

   f What are the advantages and disadvantages of students working part-time?

   g Do you like modern buildings or do you prefer them to be more old-fashioned?

   h What are the most time-consuming daily activities for you?

   i What information can non-verbal communication give us?

   j How can you ensure friendships are long-lasting?

5 🔊 2.35 Listen to check your answers. Practise saying the questions, paying particular attention to the stress in the compound adjectives.

6 With a partner, ask and answer the questions in 2. Remember to give reasons for your answers.

Exam listening

Section 4

 2.36

Questions 31–35

Complete the notes below.
*Write **NO MORE THAN TWO WORDS OR A NUMBER** for each answer.*

Procrastination: postponing tasks until a later date
Research shows 90% of Britons put off **31** ....
Aim of research: To find out:
– how procrastination affects lives
– common characteristics of procrastinators
– which tasks are **32** ....

↓

Twelve **33** .... of people who kept log of tasks, letters and emails for one week.

↓

– Subjects unaware of **34** .... of study.
– Subjects interviewed at end of week.

↓

Questionnaire created with sixteen **35** .... questions.

↓

100 people interviewed (face-to-face and by email).

↓

Results analysed.

STAGE 1

STAGE 2

 2.37

Questions 36–38.

*Choose **THREE** letters A–G.*

What type of tasks are procrastinators more likely to avoid?

A   tasks with a distant deadline

B   enjoyable tasks

C   DIY tasks

D   non-essential tasks

E   unpleasant tasks

F   tasks with an immediate deadline

G   tasks at work

Questions 39–40.

*Choose **TWO** letters A–E.*

Which people are more likely to procrastinate?

A   those with high level qualifications

B   younger age groups

C   those who lack determination and self-control

D   those who work longer hours

E   those who lack the skills to complete the task

Phonemic Chart

iː w**ee**k	ɪ th**i**n	ʊ b**oo**k	uː sh**oo**t	ɪə h**ear**	eɪ d**ay**	ː ⤴
e l**e**t	ə lat**er**	ɜː l**ear**n	ɔː f**or**	ʊə ma**ture**	ɔɪ t**oy**	əʊ fl**ow**
æ m**a**p	ʌ f**u**n	ɑː f**ar**	ɒ st**o**p	eə f**air**	aɪ l**i**ght	aʊ d**ow**n
p **p**en	b **b**ite	t **t**own	d **d**o	tʃ **ch**eck	dʒ **j**am	k **c**an	g **g**o
f **f**ight	v **v**ery	θ **Th**ursday	ð **th**ey	s **s**ame	z **z**one	ʃ **sh**ut	ʒ lei**s**ure
m **m**ale	n **n**ight	ŋ ri**ng**	h **h**ot	l **l**ike	r **r**ight	w **w**ait	j **y**ear

Answer Key

Unit 1

Topic talk

1

a A: a child starting school
  B: a couple getting married
  C: a young adult celebrating a
  significant birthday
b, c Students' own answers.

2

a voluntary work
b driving test
c family
d sabbatical
e early retirement
f gap year
g degree
h a place of your own

3

a I **do voluntary work** two afternoons
  a week at a local charity; I visit elderly
  people in my neighbourhood and do
  odd jobs for them.
b I'm very nervous as I've already failed
  twice; I really want to **pass my driving
  test** so that I can be more independent.
c We **started a family** last year so at the
  moment I'm a stay-at-home mum – it's
  hard work!
d **I'm taking a sabbatical** so that I can
  write my book; I'm also planning to
  travel to Australia. I'm so excited!
e I intend to **take early retirement** by
  the time I'm 55; I've been working
  since I was 15 so I think I'm due some
  relaxation.
f When I leave school I'm **taking a gap
  year**; I'd like to work for a few months
  to save some money and then go
  travelling.
g After three years hard work I'm finally
  going **to get my degree**; my whole
  family is coming to the ceremony.
h I'd like to be independent and **get a
  place of my own**; I'd miss my mum's
  cooking though!

4

Students' own answers.

5

a disappointing
b unremarkable
c straightforward
d ordinary
e satisfying
f dull
g insignificant

6

Positive: rewarding, fulfilling,
unforgettable, memorable, once in a
lifetime, special, satisfying, stimulating,
exciting, life-changing, momentous

Negative: disappointing, unremarkable,
tough, trying, frustrating, dull, insignificant

Nether positive or negative: challenging,
straightforward, ordinary

7–9

Students' own answers.

Listening skills

1

1 D
2 B
3 A
4 C

2

1 c
2 g
3 a
4 d
5 f
6 i
7 b
8 e
9 j
10 h

3

1 XB503
2 (dark) blue
3 £349.99
4 45
5 Jennie
6 rocks
7 (up to) 300 kgs
8 December
9 07860 643654
10 before 4 pm

4

telephone message: c, e
language school enrolment form: f, h, j
notes about a product: a, g
lecture notes: b, d, i

5

a Sunday
b skin, meat
c bike
d one
e Helen Black
f £132
g free case
h 16
i fish
j intermediate

Script

A

Shop assistant ... the cheapest model
we have is the XB503. It's very good
value and has a number of special
features, including a free case and 6
months' guarantee.
Customer Did you say XB505? I can't
see that in the catalogue.
Shop assistant No, it's the XB503. It's
on page 14.
Customer Oh yes, I see it. Mmm. That
looks interesting. What other colours
does it come in?
Shop assistant Let's see. This model is
available in standard black, as you can
see, and also white and dark blue. Oh, I
see that the white model is out of stock
at present.
Customer I like the sound of the blue
one. How much is it?
Shop assistant The price we are
currently offering is only available until
Sunday and it includes next-day delivery
... that's £349.99 altogether – that's £50
off the previous price.
Customer Great. I'll take it.
Shop assistant OK, so can I take your
name ...

B

Teacher So Yue, the result of your
entrance test is 45. That puts you in our
intermediate class.
Student Oh. In my old school I was in
the highest level.

Teacher I'm sure you'll find it's the correct level for you. See how it goes in the first few days and if there's a problem you can talk to your teacher – her name's Jennie – you'll meet her tomorrow.

Student Jennie? Can you spell that?

Teacher Yes, it's J-E-N-N-I-E.

Student J-E-N-I-E

Teacher No, it's two 'n's.

Student Oh, N-N-I-E. Thank you.

Teacher And you'll be in classroom number 12 – I'll show you where that is later. So, you've decided to do four mornings and two afternoons a week – is that right?

Student Yes, to start with. I hope to increase my hours later, would that be OK? I'd like to study full-time if possible.

Teacher Yes, that's fine. Our full-time programme is 20 hours a week but I'll put you down for 16 hours for now.

Student So how much will I have to pay?

Teacher The full-time fees are £165 a week. So for sixteen hours – it'll be, let's see ... £132.

Student So when shall I pay?

Teacher Well you can bring ...

C

Lecturer The grey seal is a large mammal found in the North Atlantic, on both sides of the ocean, so there are populations both around the British Isles and on the coast of Canada and the northern United States. They can be seen swimming out in open sea, or basking on rocks and occasionally they're spotted on sandy beaches. As already mentioned they are one of the larger mammals with the males (or bulls) weighing up to 300 kgs and over 3 metres in length. The females are usually much smaller, but even they can weigh between 100 and 200 kgs. The seals feed on a variety of fish including sand eels, cod and herring which they hunt using their highly sensitive ears and their ability to stay underwater for up to 15 minutes. Grey seals breed between September and December and produce one offspring a year, known as a pup. The young animal is born with white fur and feeds on its mother's rich milk until it is old enough to hunt. Of course the grey seal has been hunted itself, primarily for its skin, but also for its blubber or fat and its meat. At one time ...

D

Voicemail I'm not available to take your call at present. Please leave a message after the tone.

Caller Oh, hello. This is a message for Helen Black. It's about your advert in the local paper for the bike. I'm very interested in it but I have a few questions so perhaps you could call me back. My name's James Fisher and my number is 07860 643654. I'll be available most of the day on that number but I have a meeting later this afternoon, um, at 4 o'clock, so if you could call before then that would be great. Thanks.

Speaking skills

1

Possible answers

a How did you get here today?

b What do you like about your home town?

c Do you live in a house or flat?

d Do you prefer eating at home or in a restaurant?

e How long have you been learning English?

f Do you play any sports?

Script

a

I came by bus. In fact I had to take two different buses because my home is on the other side of the city and the whole journey took about 45 minutes. I like travelling by bus but I don't do it very often as I usually walk or cycle to school, which is really near my home. I only use it if I want to go on a longer journey like into the city centre. Today I had quite a long distance to travel and that's why I came by bus.

b

What I like most is the fact that it's near the coast because I love the sea. I always try to go there at weekends. I also think it has good facilities – there's plenty to do, particularly for young people as there's a leisure centre and swimming pool, two cinemas and a large shopping centre. One thing I don't like is that we don't have many parks or green spaces so there aren't many nice places to walk or play.

c

I live in a flat – most people in my city live in flats rather than houses. It's on the third floor of a small block, which is right next to the river. It's not a very big flat but I really like it mainly because it's in a good neighbourhood. Most of our neighbours have lived there for many years as it's a very popular area to live.

d

It depends on the situation. I love going out for a meal in a restaurant for a special occasion. For instance, last week I had a fantastic meal in an Italian restaurant to celebrate my friend's birthday. Still, I think overall I prefer eating at home as my mother is an excellent cook and I really enjoy having a meal with my whole family when everyone is relaxed and happy.

e

Well, I started learning it at primary school when I was about six, so I suppose you could say I've been learning it for most of my life. But I have only been studying seriously for the last two years because at my school we didn't learn much. Actually I knew a lot of grammar but when I went to Australia two years ago I realized I couldn't understand anything! That's why I decided I wanted to learn English properly and I have been having lessons ever since then.

f

Not really. I used to play basketball and a little bit of tennis at school but I'm not very interested in playing sports. I occasionally go to the gym or go running because I like to keep fit but I don't like team sports as I'm not very good at them. I sometimes watch sports on TV with my brother, who plays basketball for a local team. I often watch him play in competitions. That's why I know so much about basketball!

2

1 In fact

2 because

3 but

4 as

5 which

6 like

7 that's why

3, 4

a as, because

b like, for instance

c in fact, and, which, also, actually, who

d that's why, so

e but, still

5

Students' own answers.

6

Possible answers

a Who do you usually go shopping with? (shopping)

b How long have you lived in your present home? (accommodation)

c Do you have a job? (work)

d Have you got a big or small family? (family)

e When did you last go on holiday? (holidays)

f What do you usually do in the evenings? (daily routines)

g How often do you eat in a restaurant? (food)

h Which sports do you prefer? (interests)

i Why did you choose to study English? (studies)

j Would you prefer to watch a film at the cinema or at home? (entertainment)

7

1 j because, so, also, and

2 c but, and, also, which, but

3 h and, as, too, who, but

4 a where, and, too, so, but, like, because

8

Students' own answers.

Pronunciation

2, 3

a I'd like to get a place of my own as soon as I can.

b I hope I can take early retirement before I'm sixty.

c I'd like to start a family when I'm about thirty years old.

d Next year I'm planning to take a sabbatical so that I can travel to South America.

e I've always wanted to get a degree in electronic engineering.

f I can't afford to take a gap year unless I can get a job and save up.

Script

a I'd like to get a place of my own as soon as I can.

b I hope I can take early retirement before I'm sixty.

c I'd like to start a family when I'm about thirty years old.

d Next year I'm planning to take a sabbatical so that I can travel to South America.

e I've always wanted to get a degree in electronic engineering.

f I can't afford to take a gap year unless I can get a job and save up.

4–6

Students' own answers.

Exam listening

Questions 1–5

1 MT4 7HV

2 full-time

3 voluntary work

4 no

5 immediately

Script

Job agency assistant Good afternoon, Wright's Employment Agency, how can I help you?

Helen Oh hello, I'm calling to register with the Agency. I'm looking for work.

Job agency assistant Have you registered with us before?

Helen No, this is my first time.

Job agency assistant OK, so shall we start by taking down some details? Can I have your name please.

Helen Yes, it's Helen Shepard, that's S-H-E-P-A-R-D.

Job agency assistant S-H-E-P-E-R-D

Helen No, A-R-D

Job agency assistant Oh, sorry. Ok I've got that. And your address?

Helen 18 Henley Street

Job agency assistant Is that in Mill Town?

Helen Yes. The postcode is MT4 7HV.

Job agency assistant 7HB?

Helen No, V.

Job agency assistant OK, I've got that. And I need a contact number.

Helen My mobile is 07945 76674. That's the best number to contact me on.

Job agency assistant So, are you interested in full- or part-time work?

Helen Well, I will be looking for a part-time job in a couple of months when I start university but at the moment I'm looking for full-time work. I left school last year and took a gap year before going to university. I'd like to work for the next two months and save some money before I go.

Job agency assistant What did you do in your gap year?

Helen I did some voluntary work for six months and then for the last three months I've been travelling in south-east Asia and Australia.

Job agency assistant Mm. That sounds exciting.

Helen Yes, it was fantastic.

Job agency assistant So, I need to take down details of any work experience. You say you did some voluntary work. What did that involve?

Helen I worked at a residential school for disabled children. I really enjoyed it – the children and the rest of the staff were fantastic. My degree course is in health and social care so it really gave me good experience for that.

Job agency assistant Yes, of course. Have you any other experience?

Helen Well, er, I did a bit of waitressing work when I was at school and I spent a summer working in the King's Hotel on West Street two years ago.

Job agency assistant What were you doing there? Waitressing?

Helen No, I was a chamber maid, you know, cleaning the bedrooms.

Job agency assistant Oh yes, I did a bit of that when I was a student. OK that all seems fine. Er, you've got some experience, which is good. Just a couple more questions. Do you drive?

Helen Yes. I took my test last year but I don't have access to a car so I do rely on public transport.

Job agency assistant That shouldn't be a problem. I'll just make a note of it here – no car. And I need to know exactly when you are available and whether you'd be able to do shift work – you know, early mornings, late nights.

Helen I don't have a problem with early morning shifts. I'd prefer not to do night shifts though.

Job agency assistant And when would you be able to start?

Helen Immediately, if necessary. The sooner, the better.

Questions 6–10

6 Leisure Centre

7 meals

8 7 am–3 pm

9 disabled lady

10 £6.80

Script

Job agency assistant I'll just check our database to see if we have anything suitable. Let's see. Erm, we have some hotel work here: the Hylands. Do you know it?

Helen Is it the one near the Priors Shopping Centre?

Job agency assistant No, it's just off the ring road on the other side of town, near the Leisure Centre.

Helen Umm. That's quite a distance for me. Is it cleaning work?

Job agency assistant Well, I think it's a bit of everything. Some cleaning, some waitressing and kitchen work. It would be shift work, but nothing later than 10. The hourly rate is £6.75 with meals provided.

Helen That sounds reasonable but I'd prefer something a little closer to home if possible as that's a long journey for me.

Job agency assistant Well, we also have two positions as carers. The first one is in a residential home for the elderly. It's on Hamilton Terrace, The Cedars Care Home.

Helen Oh yes, I know where that is. It's only ten minutes' walk from my house.

Job agency assistant That's convenient, then. Er, they want someone with experience, umm, I'm not sure if your experience with children would count. I could give the manager a ring and find out.

Helen Do you know what the hours are?

Job agency assistant Yes, it says here five shifts a week from 7 am–3 pm, including some weekends. Erm, there may also be some evening shifts available. The pay is not as good as the hotel job, only £6.10 an hour.

Helen And the other one?

Job agency assistant The other one is an interesting one. It's caring for a disabled lady in her own home in Poplar Street, helping her wash and dress and doing housework and shopping for her, that sort of thing. It's not full-time work though, just two to three hours every morning. The pay is good – £6.80 an hour – and transport is provided.

Helen I do like the sound of that but I really need more hours. I think the care home sounds the most suitable.

Job agency assistant We can arrange an interview for you if you like. I'll ring the manager now and find out when he can see you. Are you available this afternoon?

Helen Yes, I'm free all day …

Unit 2

Topic talk

1
Students' own answers.

2
a retro
b over the top
c classic
d conservative
e unique
f mainstream
g functional

3
Suggested answers
a classic/unique car
a classic/contemporary/traditional/ functional design
a classic/mainstream/unique film
a classic/retro/over the top haircut
classic/contemporary/mainstream/retro fashion
contemporary/mainstream/traditional music
a classic/conservative/contemporary/ retro outfit
a functional/unique room

4
Students' own answers.

5
1 i
2 b
3 h
4 c
5 f
6 e
7 a
8 g
9 d

6
Students' own answers.

7
a on
b about
c of; to
d of
e for; over
f to
g in
h than
i of; for
j in

8
Students' own answers.

Listening skills

1
Plan A shows an outdoor arts festival (clues: *stage, field, stalls*).
Plan B shows a language department in a university (clues: *lecture theatre, seminar room, language lab*).

2
1 disabled toilets
2 first aid tent
3 camping area
4 children's play area
5 main stage
6 VIP area

3
a True
b False. As you enter seminar room **B** the staff room is directly behind you. **OR** As you enter seminar room A **the reception** is directly behind you.
c False. There are male and female cloakrooms on either side of **the main entrance**.
d True
e False. From the office to seminar room B you need to cross **the seating area**.
f False. To access the office you need to go through **the reception**.
g True

4
a the lecture theatre
b the language lab
c women's cloakroom

Script

a So, we're standing at the main entrance, so you just need to go straight down through the seating area. You'll go through some double doors into the study area and then it's first on the right.
b As you leave this office, go back through reception and you'll see the seating area to your right. You need to head across the seating area and it's the last door on your left before you get to the double doors.
c It's at the other end of the department. Go out of the lecture theatre and back through the double doors. you'll see a seating area and in front of you is the main entrance to the department. It's in the corner directly to the left of the entrance.

5
Students' own answers.

6
A school and surrounding roads.

7
Students' own answers.

8
1 C
2 E
3 F
4 B
5 A
6 G
7 D

Script

Head teacher Now, as you can see, we've put together a plan showing the school site with all the proposed changes marked. This will be distributed to all parents, teachers and residents in the surrounding streets, that is Waverley Road, Wood Lane and Lower Road. So I'll just summarize the main changes we've proposed. Firstly we plan to enlarge the school car park. As you know, parking is a problem and we would like to be able to accommodate all the staff cars as well as provide a small visitors' parking area – that would be at the Lower Road end of the current car park. We believe this measure is long overdue and will stop visitors from parking on pavements and obstructing entrances.

We also plan to install a pedestrian crossing near the side entrance in Waverley Road. The Wood Lane crossing, which was installed three years ago, has proved very popular and I'm sure you'll agree that those children and parents using the side entrance need to be kept just as safe as those using our main entrance. Over the years traffic on both roads has increased substantially and that's why we also plan to introduce traffic calming measures in Wood Lane, which probably suffers the most. This, we hope, will keep the speed down to 20 mph. New traffic signs will also be installed at the corners of both roads, warning drivers that children are crossing ahead.

As some of you might already know, it has recently been decided that the land opposite the school on the other side of Waverley Road is going to be developed into flats and offices. Although I know there was some opposition to this plan, we at the school welcome the council's decision to develop this derelict land but we need to be prepared for many months of construction work next to the school. We've therefore decided that within the next three months we're going to erect a new fence. This will run parallel to Waverley Road and we hope will screen the playground from the construction site and provide better privacy and security for the children when they're playing. Our final proposal is nothing to do with security but we hope it will bring pleasure to many people. Our plan is to establish a garden next to the playground on the Wood Lane side and Mrs Holmes has very kindly offered to supervise the project. We hope to get all the children

involved in some way and we would welcome any volunteers among staff or parents to help with any heavy digging. If you have any comments on the plans or if you would like to find out any more, please come and speak to me or one of my colleagues. We would welcome your feedback and hope to ...

Speaking skills

1
1 A an art/photographic exhibition
  B a Shakespeare play
  C a classical music concert
2, 3 Students' own answers.

2
The man is describing the classical music concert. He enjoyed the concert but didn't like the venue, which was too small.

3
a that I particularly enjoyed
b reason why I go to; because
c they showed me was
d else that really impressed me
e I didn't like was

Script

The thing that I particularly enjoyed was the violin concerto. It's one of my favourite orchestral pieces anyway but the soloist was very good – she really managed to capture the mood of the piece. The reason why I go to events like this is because I like to see local talent and these performers were all excellent. What they showed me was how good amateur musicians can be. Something else that really impressed me was the age of the musicians – they were all so young – some of them were only in their late teens and they were playing like professionals. What I didn't like was the venue. It was very small and it was difficult for the audience to see the stage. At least the acoustics were good so we could hear all right.

4, 5
See audio script.

Script

a What made this show special was the small, intimate venue.
b The thing that really impressed me was the artist's talent.
c The reason I absolutely love her designs is because they are so modern and fresh.
d Something I particularly remember is the incredible costumes and scenery.
e Something I'm not very keen on is this type of modern art.

f The thing that makes this film worth seeing is the fascinating story.
g The reason why I didn't like the book was because the story was so complicated.
h What the film made me realize was what difficult lives some people lead.

6, 7
Students' own answers.

Pronunciation

1, 2
See underlined words and phrases in audio script.

Script

a Something I <u>really didn't</u> like was the <u>noise</u>.
b The thing I <u>remember most</u> is the <u>beautiful choral piece</u>.
c What made the <u>concert special</u> was the <u>fantastic choir</u>.
d What I <u>absolutely loved</u> about the play were the <u>wonderful costumes</u>.
e The thing I <u>particularly liked</u> were the <u>stunning visual effects</u>.
f The thing that <u>really impressed</u> me was the <u>amazing script</u>.

3, 4
See underlined words and phrases in audio script.

Script

a I'm a <u>big fan</u> of <u>contemporary art</u>.
b <u>Orchestral music doesn't</u> appeal to me <u>at all</u>.
c I <u>really can't</u> see the <u>attraction</u> of the <u>latest fashion trend</u>.
d I'm <u>quite passionate</u> about <u>traditional dancing</u>.
e I'm <u>not too keen</u> on <u>folk music</u> but I <u>love this song</u>.
f I <u>absolutely love classic literature</u> but I'm <u>not too keen</u> on <u>this particular writer</u>.

5, 6
Students' own answers.

Exam listening

Questions 11–15
11 A
12 C
13 A
14 B
15 B

Script

Good evening everyone, and welcome to the new Midlands Arts Centre. We are delighted that so many of you have managed to brave the rain and come out tonight to help us celebrate the opening of this new facility. I'm here to tell you a little bit about the complex itself and show you what is on offer here. But first, a little background. It was well over fifteen years ago now that the idea was born to create a centre of drama, music and art that would attract visitors from the local area and beyond. Our aim was to provide a place of entertainment for the whole family, which would also offer education and training opportunities to performers and artists from around the world, as well as the local community. With the help of local businesses, we aim to offer annual grants to up-and-coming artists who might otherwise be unable to fulfil their dreams. As you will see when you look around, we already have an exhibition of two young local artists – you will find that in Exhibition room B. I must admit I've never been a big fan of abstract art but I was blown away by the exhibits on display by these talented youngsters. Exhibition room A houses our other temporary display. This one includes sculpture made from recycled objects and a collection of film posters from the 1970s and 80s, a must for any film buffs out there. The Rees Gallery houses our permanent exhibits, which include a collection of historical photographs of the local area and work by local artists Jemma Brock and Giles Priestman. There will be guided tours every 15 minutes throughout the evening. For any budding young artists here this evening, we have a Drawing Workshop starting in five minutes with celebrated local cartoonist, Andy Mynott. Andy will be sharing some techniques for creating caricatures and showing some of his most famous works. You will find Andy at the back of the Rees Gallery and all under 16s are welcome. There are many other events taking place this evening but I haven't got time to go through all of them – your programme will give you details. I've just picked out a few of the highlights. Later in the evening there will be a performance from the Midlands Youth Band and Dale Park Youth Choir – this is the first time they have performed together and I can guarantee that it is not to be missed. They are performing tonight in the Gilbert Theatre at 7.00 pm but don't worry if you miss that one, they will be on again at 8.45 pm, this time in the Studio. Be sure to get there in good time.

Another important event tonight is a talk by local writer, James Carver. He'll be

discussing his series of historical crime novels and reading from his latest book, *The Secret Stone*. He will also be signing copies of his books. I know he has a lot of fans out there so make sure you go along. The event starts in the Studio at 7.30 pm. Finally, the big event of the evening will be a performance by the award-winning Simon Bradford and his Jazz and Blues band. Simon has recently completed a sell-out tour of Europe and has just released a new album and we are delighted he has travelled all the way from his home in Canada for tonight's performance. His show and album have received fantastic reviews and I really can't wait for this. Be sure to be seated in the Moffat Hall in good time for the show. It starts at 9 pm and will be the final event of the evening.

Questions 16–20
16 Box Office
17 Stage Door Café
18 Temporary Exhibition Rooms
19 Studio Theatre
20 Cloakrooms

Script
Now, you should all have a programme with a plan of the complex. Please do have a good look around while you're here and make the most of the facilities. So, we're standing just by the main entrance and you can see the Moffat Hall at the back of the complex on my right. This is the main feature of the complex and seats almost 2,000. We hope this will become a world-class concert venue and one glance at the forthcoming events gives a good indication of what we can look forward to in the coming months. By the way, if you wish to book for any forthcoming events, the Box Office, which is over here on my left, will be open all evening.

There are two places to get refreshments. For light meals and snacks you can try the Stage Door Café. You'll see that straight in front us. It is open all day from 10 am and serves snacks until 9 pm. For something more substantial, you can try our Italian Restaurant which serves freshly prepared pizza, pasta and other classic Italian dishes. You'll find it on the left there next to the Box Office and it's open from midday until 11 pm. I ate there earlier and the food is absolutely delicious.

All the arts exhibits are to the right of the entrance. Access to the Temporary Exhibition rooms is around the back of the Rees Gallery. To get to these, go past the entrance to the gallery and turn

right and you'll see some double doors immediately on your right. As you go through the doors, Exhibition room A is on your right and B is on your left. Our two theatres, The Gilbert and the Studio, can both be found over there towards the back of the building. You can see the Studio, which seats 150, over there next to the cinema. Immediately to the right and behind the café is the 800-seater Gilbert Theatre. We hope that these two venues will be used by professional touring theatre companies as well as for local amateur productions. You will see as you enter the centre there is a gift shop directly on your right. This sells greetings cards, books and a variety of gifts, including paintings by local artists. Finally, I should just point out the cloakrooms. You will see the nearest are here on my left and there are further facilities near the entrance of the Moffat Hall.

Well, there's nothing more for me to say than to wish you all an enjoyable evening. If you any questions, please do ...

Unit 3

Topic talk
1
a extreme weather: floods; high temperatures; storms/high winds
b, c Students' own answers.

2
Natural disasters: b, c, e, f
Caused by human activity: a. It could be argued that human activity can also contribute to b, d and e.

3
Possible answers
Civil war can be affected by a poor harvest and an economic crisis.

Civil war can result in refugees and homelessness.

Drought can be caused by climate change and global warming.

Drought can lead to a poor harvest and a threat to endangered species.

An earthquake can result in homelessness and epidemics.

Famine can be result from a extreme temperatures and a poor harvest.

Famine can result in disease and poverty.

Flooding can be affected by deforestation and climate change.

Flooding can lead to refugees and disease.

A volcanic eruption results in homelessness and can lead to migration.

4
a disastrous
b widespread
c main
d disastrous
e trivial
f eternal
g complicated
h important

5
Questions a and f are more personal (these reflect the type of questions in Part 1 of the Speaking test). The remaining questions are more abstract (these reflect the type of questions in Part 3 of the Speaking test).

6
1 g, h
2 b, i
3 c
4 d
5 e
6 a, f

7

a 5	g 2
b 2	h 5
c 3	i 6
d 6	j 1
e 4	k 4
f 3	

8
Student's own answers.

Listening skills

1
1 a: author, journalist, novelist
   b: tutor, professor, teacher
   c: masters, PhD, doctoral (student)
2 a: half past one, one-thirty, half one
   b: one forty-five, (a) quarter to two (Br E), (a) quarter of two (Am E)
   c: two thirty, half past two, half two
3 a: refectory, dining hall
   b: coffee bar, coffee shop
   c: science block, Chemistry/Physics building

2
1 a
2 b
3 c

Script

Mel So Andrew, have you heard about the lecture on Friday?
Andrew No, I didn't know we had one on Friday.
Mel It's a special one – one of the PhD students was telling me about it. The speaker is Sheila McKee – you know the author of that book we've been reading? Well, she's giving a special lecture on global warming. Look here's a poster – 'Global Warming: Separating Fact from Fiction'. It's being organized by one of the professors in the School of Environmental Sciences, but anyone is welcome to go along.
Andrew That sounds quite interesting. Are you going?
Mel Yes, I found her book fascinating so I hope it'll be good. It starts at half past two. Do you want to meet beforehand and grab a coffee?
Andrew Well I've got a tutorial until half one. But I could meet you after that, say a quarter to two in the refectory?
Mel But the talk is in Lecture Theatre C, that's miles away. Um, why don't we meet on the ground floor of the Science block? Then we can go that little coffee bar near the Physics lab.
Andrew Then we'll be near the lecture theatre. OK, I'll see you there.

3
a author
b a quarter to two
c Science block

4
Suggested answers
4 surprised: shocked; speaker: lecturer; theories: ideas
5 support: back up; argument: case; sea levels: average height of the sea in relation to the land
6 follow: pursue

5
4 controversial
5 statistical evidence
6 blog

Script

Andrew So, what did you think of the lecture?
Mel She's such a good speaker – I'm so glad I went. What amazed me was how controversial some of her ideas were. She really did try to challenge some of our widely accepted beliefs about the subject. But she was such a powerful speaker that I found myself going along with almost everything she said.
Andrew I don't think everyone agreed with her though. Did you hear Professor Lambert at the end?
Mel Well, I think he had a point. Some of the things Mrs McKee was saying about sea levels – well she couldn't back it up. She had absolutely no statistical evidence to support it. Professor Lambert was just trying to get his opinion across.
Andrew Yes I know. The question and answer session at the end was the most entertaining part. So many people got involved and I don't think she managed to answer all the questions.
Mel Did you know she contributes regularly to *Scientist Today* and she has her own website? Now that I've read her book and heard her speak, I'm really keen to find out more. I'm definitely going to keep an eye on her blog – it should be worth reading.

6
Students' own answers.

7
A: 1820s, 1890s
B: 1940s, 1950s
C: late 20th century

1 was invented: was made up
2 increase considerably: go up noticeably
3 a decrease: a fall
4 identified: recognized/acknowledged
5 identified: recognized/acknowledged
6 high temperature records: top/highest temperatures
   broken: smashed
7 drought: lack of rain/dry weather; North America: Canada/USA
   occurred: took place

8
1 A
2 C
3 B
4 C
5 A
6 C
7 C

Script

Mel That lecture last week on global warming really got me thinking. I've decided I'm going to do my assessed presentation on global warming.
Andrew Well, there's certainly enough information on it. How are you going to narrow it down? You can't talk about the whole subject in 15 minutes.

Mel Yes, I know. I've started doing a bit of background reading and it's fascinating really. I always thought global warming was a relatively recent thing – so much of the information is about events like the Kyoto Protocol but apparently scientists were talking about it nearly two hundred years ago.

Andrew Really?

Mel Yes, I read that Jean-Baptiste Fourier made a prediction in 1827 about the earth getting warmer due to an atmospheric effect which he likened to a greenhouse. So, he is in fact credited with coining the term *the greenhouse effect*.

Andrew Ah, that's interesting. I thought it would have been later. So scientists back then were aware that there might be a problem?

Mel Well, yes and no. You see there were a few who, like Fourier, proposed that there could be a potential problem with global warming but at this stage no-one really knew that the process had already begun.

Andrew So when did they begin to realize?

Mel Well most people didn't really take the whole thing seriously until temperatures started to show a significant rise in the latter part of the 20th century.

Andrew Surely temperatures started to rise before then?

Mel Yes, of course. Throughout the earlier part of that century average temperatures were in fact rising but only very gradually and of course some scientists were monitoring the situation. They rose by 0.25°C during that period.

Andrew That doesn't sound much.

Mel Well I know it doesn't sound a huge amount but the trend was definitely upwards for 40 or so years. It didn't last though and from about 1945 onwards a lot of scientists lost any interest they might have had in global warming as the world's temperature showed a downward trend for the next few years.

Andrew Why was that?

Mel Well, most scientists reckon it was to due to emissions of aerosol sulphates from industrial and volcanic activity, which can have a cooling effect on the atmosphere.

Andrew So scientists didn't really sit up and take notice until much later?

Mel That's right. And it wasn't until 1979 that there was enough concern for the World Climate Conference to call on governments to take action to prevent further climate change through human activity. Another thing I didn't know was that greenhouses gases like methane and nitrous oxide weren't recognized as playing a part until 1985.

Andrew As late as that?

Mel Yes, I was surprised too. Way back at the end of the previous century, scientists suggested that carbon dioxide and the burning of fossil fuels could affect global temperatures and this was generally accepted throughout the twentieth century. But it was 100 years later that they discovered that actually there were other gases apart from CO_2 contributing to the greenhouse effect.

Andrew So, a lot was happening around that time?

Mel Yes, the eighties was a record-breaking decade for temperature highs. When you compare the temperatures of the coldest years in the eighties to the warmest years 100 years earlier, the 1980s were still warmer. Towards the end of the decade the USA and Canada suffered a severe drought, which killed thousands and cost around 100 billion dollars in damage. This, as well as other extreme weather events, was presented as evidence of global warming. It was only then that the world at large really became aware of what a huge issue global warming is.

Speaking skills

1, 2
Students' own answers.

3
1 agree
2 far
3 me
4 tend
5 against
6 would
7 view
8 believe

4
a 1
b 4
c 8
d 3
e 2
f 7
g 6
h 5

Pronunciation

1

Verb	Noun
exaggerate	exaggeration
pollute	pollution
justify	justification
consume	consumption
contribute	contribution
destroy	destruction
deteriorate	deterioration
emit	emission
contaminate	contamination
classify	classification
protect	protection
inform	information
conserve	conservation
present	presentation
realize	realization
populate	population
prevent	prevention
migrate	migration
reduce	reduction
recommend	recommendation

2
The stressed syllable in the nouns ending in -ion is always the penultimate syllable, as shown in the script below.

Script
ex'aggerate, exagge'ration
po'llute, po'llution
'justify, justifi'cation
con'sume, con'sumption
con'tribute, contri'bution
de'stroy, de'struction
de'teriorate, deterio'ration
e'mit, e'mission
con'taminate, contami'nation
'classify, classifi'cation
pro'tect, pro'tection
in'form, infor'mation
con'serve, conser'vation
pre'sent, presen'tation
'realize, reali'zation
'populate, popu'lation
pre'vent, pre'vention
mi'grate, mi'gration
re'duce, re'duction
reco'mmend, recommen'dation

3

a contributes

b destruction

c deterioration

d consumption

e pollution

f migration

g protect/conserve

h justify

4

Students' own answers.

Exam listening

Questions 21–25

21 B

22 C

23 A

24 A

25 B

Script

Tutor Right Mel, you wanted to see me to get some feedback on your proposal and outline for your presentation. I've had a good look through now and I've made a few notes about areas I feel you can improve. I must admit, when I first saw the topic you had chosen I was a little worried.

Mel Really?

Tutor Yes, well it can be difficult to produce something fresh and interesting when you take on a topic like climate change. So much has already been written about it and, well, it's not exactly original. But I have to say I like the way you've approached the subject matter.

Mel Thank you. Yes, I know it's a subject that has probably been chosen many times before and that's why I decided to take a slightly different angle. I decided to base the presentation on an analysis of extreme weather and natural disasters over the last few years. There seems to be plenty of information on the topic and I'll be able to include lots of visual material, photographs, graphs and so on.

Tutor Yes, I really like the idea and you've produced a clear outline of the main points. Something I am a little concerned about though is the order you plan to use them in. I'm not sure it's entirely logical. I think that needs some rethinking.

Mel Yes, I did wonder about that. Do you think the section on natural disasters should come later?

Tutor Yes, but that's not the only thing. Look, I've made some notes and suggested a possible order.

Mel Mmm. Yes, I see what you mean. I did wonder whether I needed to add a section about the recent flooding in parts of Europe?

Tutor Well I think you should definitely mention it but I'm not sure it needs its own section. What about including it in the introduction? In my opinion the introduction is the weakest part – it needs much more substance.

Mel Yes, I wasn't sure what to include.

Tutor Well, you need to grab your audience's attention at the start. And then you should include some background information on the topic and outline your main points.

Mel And what's the best way of getting their attention?

Tutor Well, it could be a surprising or interesting fact, a picture, or an anecdote.

Mel I know. I found some fantastic pictures on the Internet of the flooding. If I can find some statistics about it too, would that be a good way to start?

Tutor Absolutely. It will show the audience the relevance of your presentation and bring it right up to date. Remember to check the copyright and acknowledge your sources for any visual material you use.

Mel Really? For pictures? I didn't realize I had to.

Tutor Yes, you should acknowledge all your sources in your bibliography and on your slides too.

Mel Well, I've already started my bibliography.

Tutor Yes, I looked at that.

Mel Is there a problem?

Tutor Not exactly. It's good to see you're taking a note of your sources but there's so many of them and I'm not sure about the validity of some of these internet sources.

Mel How do you mean?

Tutor Well, take this graph you've found about rainfall. Couldn't you find a more reliable source? This is taken from someone's blog! You need to make sure all your information is from trusted sources – academic papers, scientific journals, that sort of thing.

Mel OK. And I need to cut the number of entries in my bibliography?

Tutor Only include the sources you actually use and refer to in your presentation. I would say no more than about ten for this assignment.

Questions 26–30

26 animation

27 eye contact

28 wireless

29 memory aid

30 questions

Script

Tutor OK, so, you're happy with the organization and content, plenty to work on there. Now I believe you had some questions about the actual delivery of the presentation?

Mel Yes, well it's more the technical side of things really. I'm not very confident with the equipment and I've never given a presentation before so I'm really nervous.

Tutor Well, I think the best way to overcome your nerves is by preparing really thoroughly. Make sure you know the subject matter inside out and that any visual aids and equipment are ready.

Mel Yes. I wanted to ask about that. I'm getting a friend to help me put together the slides – have you any advice about that?

Tutor The one thing I would say is don't put too much information on your slides, just the main points and any relevant visuals. You want your slides to support what you're saying. And I would also keep the slides themselves very simple – no fancy colours or animation that will distract the audience from what you're saying.

Mel No sound effects then?

Tutor No, definitely not. And what you need to do is practise. You'll feel far more confident if you've run through it a few times with a friend.

Mel My friend is going to listen to me run through it.

Tutor On the actual day of the presentation, there are a few important things to remember. First, think about where you stand. It's vital that you position yourself centrally and make eye contact with your whole audience – don't forget the people sitting at the sides. If you smile and look friendly, it will make your audience feel relaxed too. And don't fidget and move around too much – it can be very distracting.

Mel What about my slide show? I'll need to be near the computer to move the slides forward.

Tutor Have you thought about using a wireless mouse or keyboard? That will really help – it means you can control the slide show without having to move or turn your back on the audience every time you change slides.

Mel That's a good idea – I hadn't thought of that.

Tutor The other thing to remember is that when we're nervous, we tend to speak more quickly so make a real effort to speak calmly and clearly so that your audience understands you and doesn't feel rushed.

Mel What about memorizing the talk? A friend told me she did that for her presentation but I don't think she did terribly well.

Tutor No, it's not a very good idea. It will make you sound unnatural. And don't read from a prepared speech because that will also affect the delivery and stop you making eye contact. Why don't you try using cue cards? You can include all the main points and any key facts or numbers as a memory aid – it will sound far more natural.

Mel Mm. The other thing I'm a little worried about is questions from the audience. Should I answer them immediately or wait 'til the end?

Tutor The best thing to do is tell the audience in the introduction that you will answer their questions at the end of the presentation. That way you won't get any distracting interruptions. If you're not sure about the answer, ask the questioner to repeat the question – that will give you thinking time. You could always direct the question back to the questioner or the audience – asking them what they think.

Mel Great. Thanks for all your advice – it's been really helpful.

Tutor No problem. I'm looking forward to your presentation.

Unit 4

Topic talk

1

Students' own answers.

2

a Minority
b first
c cross-cultural
d Face-to-face
e common
f second
g dead
h written
i official
j non-verbal

3

strong agreement: g, h, i
cautious agreement: b, e, f
cautious disagreement: a, j
strong disagreement: c, d

4

1 e
2 c
3 a
4 i
5 f
6 b
7 j
8 d
9 g
10 h

5

1 cautious disagreement
2 strong agreement
3 strong agreement
4 cautious agreement
5 cautious disagreement
6 cautious disagreement
7 strong agreement
8 strong disagreement
9 strong disagreement
10 strong agreement

6

Students' own answers.

Listening skills

1

a Europe.
b Rare languages – the figures on the bar charts indicate there are not many speakers of these languages.
c Suggested answers
  A shows north-west England, Northern Ireland and an island off the southern coast of England.
  B shows Scotland, Wales and Republic of Ireland.
  C shows south-west England, north-west France and an island between north-west England and Ireland.
d Students' own answers.

2

1 C
2 B (The current number of native speakers is difficult to estimate but it's clear that Breton has somewhere in the region of 200,000; there are significantly more non-native speakers of all three languages with Breton having as many as 300,000 able to speak or write it to some level.)

3 A (It's a similar story with Manx, with around 2,000 speaking it as a second language, a far healthier figure than the number of native speakers, which could be as few as 100.)

Script

Today's lecture is the first in a series of lectures about minority languages. We are going to look at a number of languages from across the globe but today I'm going to start closer to home with a look at some of the Celtic languages, which are mainly but not exclusively spoken in north-western Europe.

As you can see from the shaded areas of this map, apart from the clearly defined areas of Scotland, Ireland and Wales where we have speakers of Scots Gaelic, Irish and Welsh respectively, there are further pockets of other minority Celtic languages in other parts of Europe. First, we have Cornish in the south-western tip of England, Breton in the Brittany region in the north-west of France and Manx, a language spoken exclusively by people in the Isle of Man, an island located in the Irish Sea off the north-west coast of England. It is these last three languages that my talk will focus on today.

The current number of native speakers is difficult to estimate but it's clear that Breton has somewhere in the region of 200,000, which is far more than both Cornish and Manx put together. Compare this to the tiny number of Cornish native speakers – 600 or so according to some estimates. These numbers are difficult to verify, but what we do know is that there are significantly more non-native speakers of all three languages, with Breton having as many as 300,000 able to speak or write it to some level. Cornish also has far more non-native speakers, around 3,000, that's five times as many as those who speak it as their first language. It is encouraging to see larger numbers of non-native speakers like this, but as you can see numbers are still very small and a matter of concern. It's a similar story with Manx, with around 2,000 speaking it as a second language, a far healthier figure than the number of native speakers, which could be as few as 100.

3

a More detailed information about each language, including information about their decline and revival and current official and UNESCO status.

b The numbers read across, which means that each language will be dealt with separately.

c 4: a year or period of time

 5: a noun phrase describing the official status of Cornish

 6: the subject of the verb *died*, probably a person

 7: an example of how Manx is reviving

 8: a time period – part of the 20th century

 9: a past participle to describe Breton's official status

 10: a phrase describing Breton's UNESCO status.

4

4 13th century

5 minority language

6 Last native speaker

7 Increased signage

8 second half

9 Not recognized

10 Severely endangered

Script

So, let's take a closer look at these three languages. All three have declined to different extents over the centuries for various social, geographical and political reasons, which we'll cover in more detail in the next lecture. What I'd like to discuss briefly now are the attempts to revive all three of these languages from, in the case of Cornish and Manx, almost complete extinction.

At its peak Cornish had about 39,000 speakers. That was way back in the 13th century and by the mid-16th century the language was in rapid decline. It was still used in some western communities until the late 1700s and there are records of it having been used in some Cornish families as late as the 19th century. The revival process started in the early 20th century, with Cornish literature being published and music and even film being revived. A very tiny minority of Cornish children are currently being brought up bilingual and the language is taught in some schools. It was officially recognized as a UK minority language in 2002 and this led to some standardization of the various written forms which had

caused a number of disputes since the revival began. In 2010, Cornish speakers welcomed the reclassification of their language by UNESCO from an extinct language to a revitalized but critically endangered one.

Manx holds a similar UNESCO status. It suffered a steep decline during the 1800s in favour of English, which was regarded with much greater prestige and by the 1920s only a tiny percentage of islanders claimed to speak it. It was finally considered extinct in 1974, when its last native speaker died. Since then there has been a revival on the Isle of Man, which has been helped by the amount of written and audio material available. Manx is now taught as a second language in all the island's schools and there are now a number of children who can be classed as native speakers. The island has also seen increased signage and Radio Manx broadcasts a number of programmes in the traditional language. Since 1985 it has held official language status in the Isle of Man, alongside English.

Breton meanwhile suffered a similar severe decline in the second half of the 20th century and by the first decade of the 21st century, numbers of native speakers had reduced to around a fifth of the one million speakers there were in 1950 and most of these were over the age of sixty. In recent years though, the number of children attending Breton language schools where children receive all instruction in Breton up to the age of seven, has increased. Breton also has a number of publications and many translations, including the comic series, Asterix. Despite quite a strong and growing body of literature and media and a comparatively large number of speakers, Breton is not recognized as an official language in France. This is due to an article in the French Constitution which states that only French can be officially recognized. Despite the efforts of autonomists and organizations like the Breton Language Agency, which was set up in 1999 to promote the language, Breton remains a vulnerable language, and is officially classified by UNESCO as severely endangered.

Now, let's move on to look at some of the features of each language. If you look at the grammar ...

Speaking skills

1, 2

Students' own answers.

3

a to describe a letter you have been sent

b The task is about an event in the past, so most of the verbs will be in past tense, particularly past simple.

4

Who it was from: boss.

When he received it: last year.

What it was about: offering me a job.

Why it was important: really wanted the job.

Script

I'd like to talk about a letter I received last year. It was a formal letter offering me a job so it was actually from my current boss. I had been to an interview a few weeks before for a job at an advertising agency. I really wanted the job and I liked the company because although it was quite small, everyone was really friendly and the job sounded just what I was looking for. I suppose it had been about two or three weeks since I had the interview and because I didn't think I'd done well in the interview I didn't think I had got the job. In fact, I remember I admitted to my family that I hadn't got it and I started applying for other similar jobs. So when I received the letter and realized who it was from I immediately thought that it was a rejection letter. I almost didn't carry on reading it. It wasn't until I started reading it properly that I realized that they were actually offering me the job. I was so surprised that I had to read it again just to make sure I hadn't made a mistake! The letter itself was quite short. What I mean to say is it didn't say much except to offer me the job and I think there were some details about the start date and pay. I think it also invited me to go and meet everyone in the office and to sort out my contract. What I remember most is being so excited as it was my first job offer and as I said before I really hadn't expected it so it was a nice surprise because most of the letters I receive are bills and other boring letters like that. I started the job a few weeks later and I still work there now. It was definitely an important letter for me.

5

Extra details: formal letter; interview a few weeks before; didn't think I had got the job; thought it was rejection letter; surprised; short letter; details about start date and pay; invited to go to office; excited; first job offer; nice surprise.

6

All the main points are included, although the candidate didn't mention the HR department or the month that the interview took place. He doesn't say that he was pleased although it is clear that he was as he says it was a nice surprise.

7

a A person you communicate with regularly (e.g. by phone, text, letter, email).

b As it is describing an activity you do on a regular basis most of the verbs will be in the present simple.

8

Students' own answers.

Pronunciation

1

a letter I

b to an

c I admitted

d carry on

e letter itself

f so excited

Script

a I'd like to talk about a letter I received last year.

b I had been to an interview a few weeks before ...

c I remember I admitted to my family that I hadn't got it ...

d I almost didn't carry on reading it!

e The letter itself was quite short.

f What I remember most is being so excited as it was my first job offer ...

2

a /r/

b /w/

c /j/

d /j/

e /r/

f /w/

3, 4

See linking marks in audio script.

Script

a How /w/ often do you check your /r/ email inbox? Do you think this is too /w/ often?

b Are there /r/ any minority languages in your country? Are they /j/ in danger /r/ of extinction?

c How /w/ effective are your /r/ oral communication skills? What can you do to /w/ improve them?

d Does mobile technology make it easier /r/ or more difficult to switch off from study /j/ or work?

e Is your /r/ own language difficult for /r/ other language speakers to learn?

f How /w/ are languages best learnt? Are they /j/ easier to learn when you /w/ are young?

5

Students' own answers.

Exam listening

Questions 31–38

31 A

32 B

33 B

34 A

35 A

36 B

37 B

Script

Good morning everyone. I've been invited here today to talk a little about the research I've been doing into quite a modern form of communication – text messaging. I'm sure most of you here today will've already sent and received at least one text message today. It has become the most popular form of communication between friends and family, despite strong competition from social networking and email. We now send around eight trillion text messages every year, which is amazing when you think that the first text message was only sent in 1992. Over half of British people now use a smart phone and of those, over 92% choose texting as their preferred method of communication. And well over half of British people text every day compared to only 47% who make a daily phone call. That's about 50 texts a week for the average person, which might sound a lot but is comparatively few compared to other parts of the world. Unsurprisingly, it is young people who send the most texts. Amongst 18–25 year olds the average is 133 messages a week which is more than double any other age group. And whilst 15% of the over-65s say they communicate by text on a daily basis, for the youngest age group this figure rises to nine out of ten. And it is this age group who prefer to message friends, compared to the older generation whose main text recipients are family members. Apparently, men text more than women do and have a larger number of contacts that they regularly text. But they tend to be more functional in their texting and keep their texts short. Compare this to women, who send fewer texts but are more likely to send long ones in which they cultivate friendships and relationships. More than half of women questioned are happy to discuss relationship issues and even express their love through a text message.

For many of you a time without text messaging might seem a dim and distant memory. In fact it was back in December 1992 that the first ever text message was sent via the Vodafone telephone network from a PC to a telephone. The message was a simple greeting 'Merry Christmas'. The original idea was to use texting as a quick and easy way to communicate within a company, a bit like paging. In fact, it wasn't until 1994 that the first commercial text messaging service was introduced by a mobile network and even then consumer interest was very low. It was not until 1993 that the first text messaging service was launched in Sweden. A year later Vodafone introduced texting to the UK. At first texters were only able to text someone within the same network and it wasn't until 1999 that there was full compatibility between mobile networks. At first texting was quite a long and laborious task as predictive texting was not introduced until 1995. Another characteristic of early texting was that each message had to be short, at 160 characters or fewer. This limitation on length is what spawned the common shorthand used by texters the world over. Abbreviations like BTW for 'by the way' and TTYL for 'talk to you later' have now entered the English language for good, whether we like them or not. Fears that this text-speak would have an adverse effect on children's language skills have so far proven incorrect. In fact, a recent study has shown that children who are fluent in text messaging have higher than average literacy skills compared to those who don't text.

Questions 38–40

38–40 A, D, F

Script

In the early days, it would have been difficult to imagine what a versatile communication tool text messaging would become. Think about what you can use texting for. For my research I asked a sample of people of all ages about the text messages they had sent and received on a given day. Apart from the normal social chit chat, it was clear that our reliance on text messaging for everyday tasks is growing. In one day respondents to my survey used texting to track a parcel being delivered, to vote on a TV talent show, to check the status of a plane, to give money to charity, to remind them of a dentist's appointment, to confirm a hotel booking, to enter a TV contest – the list goes on and on. Texting has also been responsible for spreading information and organizing revolutionary activity and there have been numerous accounts of how text messaging has saved lives including the doctor in a remote part of Africa who saved a child's life by following instructions sent by text. But let's not forget the downside to text messaging. This type of communication has also brought us cyber bullying and has added to the dangers on the road. There has been a notable increase in recent years of road traffic accidents caused by inattention by both drivers and pedestrians whilst texting.

So what about the future? Well, with new ways of communicating appearing all the time, the future of the traditional text message seems uncertain. What is certain though is that the text message has made an indelible mark on modern communication.

Unit 5

Topic talk

1
Students' own answers.

2
1 healthy
2 unhealthy
3 healthy
4 unhealthy
5 either
6 either
7 unhealthy
8 healthy

3
a 7
b 4
c 5
d 8
e 6
f 3
g 2
h 1

4
a pasta, rice, wholemeal bread
b eggs, lentils, liver, oily fish
c green vegetables, lentils, wholemeal bread
d berries, citrus fruit, green vegetables, liver, nuts, oily fish
e butter, chocolate, eggs
f fizzy drinks, ready meals
g chocolate, ready meals, butter, nuts

5
Examples include:
a cereal, potatoes
b meat, poultry
c beans, pulses
d fruit juice, dried fruit
e cream, milk
f flavoured water, sugar
g cake, cheese

6
a food poisoning
b hyperactivity
c high blood pressure
d Tooth decay
e heart disease
f indigestion
g malnutrition
h obesity

7
Suggested answers
a Vegetarian/vegan food is low in fat, but it is more difficult to eat a balanced diet, especially if dairy products are avoided.
b Low-fat foods are healthier and less fattening but might not be so good for particular groups of people, e.g. growing children. They also might not taste as good as high-fat foods.
c Organic fruit and vegetables are free from chemicals so are healthier and better for the environment. However, they might be more expensive than non-organic and less available.
d Free-range meat and eggs are from animals who have been allowed to move around freely so are ethically more acceptable than meat or eggs from animals who have been confined. However, they are usually more expensive.

Listening skills

1
a Text B is more informal; Text A is more formal and academic.
b Text A uses more noun phrases. Examples: *the variety and availability of food; more customer choice; global population growth; increasing environmental concerns; doubts about the long-term feasibility of maintaining supplies of basic foodstuffs; increased research into new foods and farming methods.*

2
Suggested answers
a The rapid increase in obesity is causing concern among doctors.
b The development of farming methods has led to increased crop production.
c A diet high in fish oil can lead to an increase in levels of concentration.
d There may be a lack of protein in a vegetarian diet.
e There is a growing tendency for young people to take extreme measures to achieve weight loss.
f An increased interest in foreign cuisine has led to improved availability of unusual ingredients in supermarkets.

3
a Children, a poor diet, inferior
b maternal age
c Children, unhealthy diet, lack
d Rapid brain growth, declines

4
Suggested answers
1 a poor diet: children who do not eat well/eat too much fatty food/eat unhealthily
2 maternal age: the mother's age/how old the mother is
3 a lack of: don't have
4 rapid brain growth: the brain grows quickly

5
1 intellectual ability
2 level of education
3 vitamins and minerals
4 three

6
1 children who eat too much junk food and sweet things at an early age have a lower intellectual ability
2 they looked at how old the mother was and her level of education
3 The children who ate only junk and fast food didn't get enough vitamins and minerals
4 When a child is three his brain stops growing so rapidly

Script

Frank Have you had a think about this project we've got to do, Ana? I don't feel very inspired about the subject. Food and diet – I've no idea what to do.

Ana Actually, I read an interesting article yesterday which I think might give us the basis for a really interesting research area.

Frank Oh yes? What's it about?

Ana Well, according to some research children who eat too much junk food and sweet things at an early age have a lower intellectual ability when tested at the age of eight.

Frank Really? That's interesting. What else did it say?

Ana Well, apparently it's the first time a link has been found between the diet of children and their brain power in later life.

Frank But surely there are other factors involved – the way you're educated and brought up, for example.

Ana Of course, and the researchers took lots of other factors into account. They looked at how old the mother was and her level of education, as well as whether the child was breast- or bottle-fed. They also studied the home environment of the child and looked at how much access they had to toys and books. Making allowances for all these factors, they still had evidence that what you eat in the first three years of life is crucial in brain development.

Frank I suppose that's when the brain grows fastest?

Ana Exactly. The researchers looked at children with three different types of diet. Children who lived on a diet of fast food and processed foods full of additives had an IQ up to 5 points lower than the children who either had a healthy diet, or what they call a more traditional diet, as both of these included fresh fruit and vegetables. The children who ate only junk and fast food didn't get enough vitamins and minerals which maintain healthy growth, so this meant their brains never got the chance to reach their full potential.

Frank But surely you can change your diet later in life and improve your IQ?

Ana Well, apparently the damage has already been done. When a child is three his brain stops growing so rapidly, so it's vital that a child gets appropriate nutrition from an early age.

Frank You're right this is interesting. Do you think we could do something about this for our project?

Ana Well, why don't we speak to some parents and find out what they think?

Speaking skills

1

Students' own answers.

2

1 b
2 f
3 a
4 h
5 d
6 g
7 e
8 c

3

1 h
2 e
3 a
4 g
5 f
6 d
7 c
8 b

4

Possible questions

1 What's your opinion of the diet industry?
2 Do you think it is helpful to divide foods into different groups?
3 Why do you think different countries and cultures have different diets?
4 How do you think eating habits will change in the future?
5 What do you think of fast food?

5

Speaker 1: question 2
Speaker 2: question 3
Speaker 3: question 7
Speaker 4: question 8

Script

1 I think it depends on how long ago in the past you're referring to but in general, I think our modern-day eating habits are healthier than they were 100 years ago. For one thing we have far greater access to fresh and healthy foods and we also have more knowledge about what is good for us and what isn't. I suppose the reason why so many people don't have a healthy diet is they make the wrong choices and overindulge.

2 It's hard to say really. There are so many diets which claim that you can lose a lot of weight very quickly by eating strange things or cutting out certain foods. But I think extreme diets like this don't work and can be dangerous. I'm not sure what the answer is. I suppose the only healthy way to lose weight is to maintain a balanced and healthy diet and do more exercise.

3 I've never really considered this before. I guess it could have something to do with additives in food like colourings and preservatives. I think some people claim that a rise in food allergies is due to environmental factors but I'm not sure what exactly. It might be related to chemicals used in farming and food production.

4 I'm not quite sure what you mean by dietary supplements. Do you mean taking vitamin pills? Well, I think some people take them for a specific health problem or to avoid illness. But I believe if you follow a healthy diet there is no need to take extra vitamins and minerals as these can all be found in the food you eat.

6

Asking for clarification: *I'm not quite sure what you mean by ...*; *Do you mean ...?*
Gaining thinking time: *I think it depends on ...*; *I suppose*; *It's hard to say really*; *I'm not sure what the answer is*; *I've never really considered this before*

7

Possible answers

Asking for clarification: *If I understand you correctly, you're saying that ...* ; *So what you're saying is that ...* ; *Could you give me an example of ...?* ; *I didn't understand what you meant by ...*

Gaining thinking time: *I think it depends on ...* ; *I suppose*; *It's hard to say really*; *I'm not sure what the answer is*; *Well, you could say ...* ; *I don't really know*; *That's a good question*; *I'm glad you asked me that.*

8

Students' own answers.

Pronunciation

1

Students' own answers.

2

a 'd like; had
b was; had planned
c was; 'd been wanting; opened; was
d hadn't been; weren't; 'd been told; was
e had; is; 'd had; was
f 've; heard; 're closing; 'll have opened

3

All main verbs are strong. The auxiliary and modal verbs are weak. *had* is used as a main verb in a (*a meal I had*) and e (*I had lasagne*) and as an auxiliary verb elsewhere.

Script

<u>Underlined</u> verbs are weak, **bold** verbs are strong.

a I<u>'d</u> **like** to tell you about a special meal I **had** recently.

b It <u>was</u> my birthday and my friends <u>had</u> **planned** a surprise evening out for me.

c It <u>was</u> a restaurant I<u>'d been</u> **wanting** to go to ever since it **opened** so I <u>was</u> very **excited**.

d We **hadn't** <u>been</u> there before so we **weren't** sure what to expect but we<u>'d been</u> **told** it <u>was</u> very good.

e For my main course, I **had** lasagne, which <u>is</u> a dish I<u>'d</u> **had** many times before, but this one <u>was</u> absolutely outstanding.

f I<u>'ve</u> just **heard** that they<u>'re</u> **closing** in a few weeks time to redecorate but I <u>think</u> they<u>'ll have</u> **opened** again by New Year.

4

a I<u>'ll have</u> been there by then.

b I<u>'ve been</u> looking forward to going there.

c I <u>was</u> told to order the fish.

d We <u>were</u> given a free drink.

e I<u>'ve</u> never been there before.

f They<u>'re</u> offering a discount.

g I wasn't sure what they <u>were</u> doing.

h I<u>'d</u> like to <u>have</u> been there.

Exam listening

Questions 11–15

11 famous Irish dishes
12 2 pm
13 €8.50
14 8 pm
15 Irish folk singer

Script

Good morning everyone, and welcome to Ireland. It's great to see so many of you here today and I'm delighted that you have decided to join us here at the Castle Hotel for our special food lovers' weekend. Before I tell you about the main events we have planned for you, I'd just like to point out that tea and coffee and biscuits are available at the back of the room, so please help yourselves.

So, the weekend's events start straight after lunch, which you can take either in the main restaurant to my right or in the garden terrace, which you'll find to the right of the main reception desk.

This afternoon we are very excited to welcome local chef Laura Gallagher to the Castle Hotel. Laura will be showing you some typically Irish ingredients, many from her own garden, and explaining how good food needn't cost a fortune. She's also going to demonstrate a few famous Irish dishes including Irish stew. As you may know, Laura runs her own award-winning organic restaurant about ten miles from here and I know a few of you are planning to eat there tomorrow night – I can highly recommend it. So, those of you who have booked for this afternoon's session should gather in the demonstration kitchen, which is to the left of the main restaurant, by 1.45 pm so that we can get going promptly at 2 pm. And I'm sorry – a few people have already asked me but this session is now full. However, there are still places on the city bus tour, which will be leaving the hotel at 1.45. This will take you to all the main sights and there will be a chance to stop off at the Riverside Museum and café later in the afternoon. The coach will return from the museum at 5 pm promptly. Please note that entrance to the museum is not included so you will have to pay on the door – but we do have a special discount so that will be €8.50 rather than the usual €11.75.

Tonight, we have our five-course seafood dinner in the main restaurant. Our head chef has really planned a treat for you – I've seen the menu and it looks fantastic. Please note that this is not at 7.30 as originally stated in your holiday itinerary but at 8 pm. There is a seating plan up in the main reception so please check this before this evening so you know where you're seated. Oh, and one other thing regarding food – I've already had a couple of special requests from allergy sufferers so please do let me know as soon as possible if you have any special dietary requirements. After dinner, starting around 10 pm, if you still have the energy, we have Irish folk singer James Corrigan here to entertain you until the wee small hours. His family have been making Irish music for over 200 years and he will treat you to both traditional and modern folk songs. He plays no fewer than six different instruments including the bodhran, a traditional drum, the tin whistle and the Irish fiddle. Well worth staying up for!

Questions 16–20

16–18 A, E, F
19–20 B, D

Script

Tomorrow will be an early start for most of you who have booked on our culinary tour of the region. The restaurant will be open for an early breakfast from 6.30 am and the coach will be leaving at 7.45 am. We have a packed itinerary and our first stop is at Mill Farm, where they still use traditional methods to make butter, cheese and other dairy products. You will have a chance to try your hand at churning the butter and shaping it using traditional butter beaters. Our next stop is the world famous Oyster Café where you can sample fresh oysters and other shellfish. I'm hoping the weather stays fine for this as it's such a beautiful setting next to the harbour wall and you may be able to see some of the fishing boats coming in with their catch. That will just be a brief stop as the highlight of the morning will be our stop at the famous Mount Rees Baking School, where chef Jonathan Park will be showing you how to make Irish bread and giving you some other baking tips. I'm told that Jonathan has a few surprises up his sleeve and I know that he's keen on audience participation so be prepared to get your aprons on and hands dirty for that one. Our lunch stop will be the Waterside Restaurant. It's a beautiful lakeside setting and if the weather's fine you'll be able to walk around the lake after your meal. Although lunch isn't included in the trip, the restaurant is offering you the special price of a two course meal at only €25 per person. Our route home takes us through some amazing mountainous landscape and there will be chances to stop and take photographs before our final stop at the Wakeford Food Centre, which is a true retail paradise for food lovers. They sell all sorts of exotic and local ingredients and there are always plenty of tasting opportunities. Be prepared to part company with some of your euros! We aim to arrive at the centre in time for afternoon tea, if you can manage any after your lunch. Our return to the hotel will hopefully be by 6.30 pm and there will be a chance to relax for a while before dinner at 8 pm.

And so to Monday. Well, the trip to the local Farmer's market still has a number of free places so please let me know if you're interested. The price for transport there and back is €5 but of course you'll need to take along plenty of cash for all your purchases. Unfortunately we have had to cancel the talk from cookery writer

Maria Kelly as she is unwell, but instead, for those of you who are having the cookery demonstration this afternoon, we are offering you a chance to visit the Riverside Museum. Or you may just decide to spend Monday morning relaxing and enjoying the grounds here at the Castle Hotel. Lunch will be at 12.30 and then the coach to take you to the airport will leave here at 2.30.

Unit 6

Topic talk

1

Possible answers

a Design and structure of buildings; creating new building materials; ensuring safety on building site; creating and testing drugs; medical tests and research; building medical equipment.

b All areas of life, e.g. transport, farming, energy production, food production, communication.

c Creativity, imagination, mathematical skills, precision, attention to detail, logical thinking, team work.

2

1 f
2 b
3 a
4 d
5 i
6 j
7 e
8 g
9 c
10 h

3, 4

Students' own answers.

5

biology: biological
chemistry: chemical
physics: physical
psychology: psychological
botany: botanical
astronomy: astronomical
sociology: sociological
geology: geological
meteorology: meteorological
ecology: ecological

6

Possible answers

a architecture, structural engineering
b telecommunications, the internet
c farm machinery, food preservation
d drugs, medical equipment

e earthquake detection, building materials
f designing vehicles, researching new fuels
g manufacturing technology, computers
h electricity, fuel technology

7

a 7
b 8
c 6
d 9
e 2
f 10
g 5
h 4
i 1
j 3

8, 9

Students' own answers.

Listening skills

1

a tutor; postgraduate student; article; scientific journal

b tutor: lecturer, teacher
postgraduate student: master's student
article: piece, item
scientific journal: science magazine/ periodical

2

a C

b Distractors: *a friend who studies chemistry* (the friend mentioned is Dan's, not his tutor's); *her tutor* (the tutor mentioned is the friend's, not Dan's); *postgraduate engineering students* (the postgraduate students mentioned refer to the numbers in the article Dan reads, not Dan himself)

3

A academic staff: lecturers, tutors, academics

B undergraduate students: first/second year students; other countries: abroad, overseas

C postgraduate students: master's students; overseas: abroad, in other countries

4

B

Script

Dan One of the first things I did was to conduct a survey in my department and two overseas: one in China, the other in Russia. For this I enlisted the help of some members of staff and the international students in my department, who used their contacts overseas to provide me with a big enough sample. I wanted to include both first year students

and those on taught Master's degrees, although unfortunately I was unable to get responses from students on Master's programmes in either China or Russia. I had originally planned to question some of the academics working in the department, but this approach proved too complicated and so in the end I settled for only students. I did manage to get a good sample of first year students in all three countries and a small number of these are overseas students from five different countries, who are currently studying here in this department.

5

Distractors: members of staff; those on taught Master's degrees; students on Master's programmes in either China or Russia; academics working in the department

Dan mentions all of the options but says he was *unable to get responses from students on Master's programmes overseas* (C) and talking to staff *was too complicated* (A). For the correct answer (B), he says he managed *to get a good sample of first year students ... and a small number of these are overseas students.*

6

1 F
2 A
3 C
4 E

Script

I encountered a few problems with some of the participants in my survey. All the interviews were either conducted face-to-face, or in the case of overseas respondents, by telephone or Skype. One Chinese student, whom I was particularly keen to interview, as she is one of only three overseas students doing a Masters degree, proved extremely difficult to pin down. I made a number of appointments to meet her but each time she didn't show up and nobody seemed to know where I could find her. Eventually, I did manage to track her down and interview her. On one occasion when I was in the middle of an online interview with a student at university in Russia, her boyfriend interrupted and cut me off – I think he thought I was trying to steal his girlfriend! I eventually managed to complete the interview on another day. I also had a few problems with participants refusing to answer some of the questions. For example one of the first year students here was not keen to tell me his exam results or his reasons for choosing engineering – I couldn't really work out why. That was very annoying as it meant I couldn't include his answers in my final report.

Some students were downright difficult. One of the postgraduates that my tutor put me in touch with was very wary of me and didn't seem to trust me at all. He seemed convinced that I was something to do with the university staff and that his answers would affect his final results! Eventually my tutor convinced him that I was genuine.

Speaking skills

1

a gadget
b unusual
c current
d movement
e modern
f new

2

Possible answer

scientific breakthrough/groundbreaking discovery/medical research

3

Students' own answers.

4

Part 1: Questions 1, 4, 7, 8
Part 3: Questions 2, 3, 5, 6, 9, 10

5

a Question 2.
b Candidate B provides the best answer as it gives more general information, supported by examples. Candidate A's answer is too personal.
c In general; tends to; is liable to
d Candidate B supports the generalizations with specific examples (*Health and medicine would be a good example*; *Take the Internet for instance*).

6

Candidate C is answering Question 6. Language used: *on the whole*; *It often seems to be the case*.
Candidate D is answering Question 3. Language used: *As a rule*; *most jobs*; *in many cases*; *Generally speakin*; *it's more likely to be*; *they can have a tendency to*.

7

Students' own answers.

Pronunciation

1

Candidate A sounds more interested than Candidate B, who sounds uninterested due to her flat intonation. Candidate A

stresses key words and his voice rises on some of the key words (*really, actually, round, solves, far*) to show that he is engaged and interested.

Script

Examiner Do you think new developments in science often cause more problems than they solve?

Candidate A No, not really. Actually, I would say, that it's the other way round – the problems that science solves far outweigh the problems that it may bring.

Candidate B Yes, I think so. Scientific developments often cause lots of problems so sometimes they're not worth it.

2

See intonation marks in audio script.

Script

Candidate C Absolutely. I mean scientific development can be a positive thing but you need to remember all the negative consequences it can have.

Candidate D Well, I suppose it can cause problems, but overall, surely scientific development is a positive thing?

3

Students' own answers.

4

See intonation marks in audio script.

Script

a Absolutely. I don't think anyone should try to interfere with nature.

b I'm not sure really. Most research is beneficial but some can be unethical or even dangerous.

c I really don't think so. Scientists should be free to do what they like.

d It's a difficult one. If you start prohibiting some research, where do you draw the line?

e Of course, there should be some sort of guidelines otherwise scientists would do whatever they liked.

f I agree that there should be some restrictions but it's so difficult to monitor.

5

Students' own answers.

Exam listening

Questions 31–34

31 B
32 B
33 A
34 C

Script

Lecturer Today, in the first in the series of talks about significant numbers, I'm going to talk about pi. As a mathematician and engineer, I find many numbers fascinating but for me pi is probably the most interesting.

So, what is pi? Well, as all of you will probably know, pi is what you get if you divide the circumference of a circle (that's the distance around the outside edge) by its diameter (that's a straight line through its centre). And as most of you will also have learnt in your maths lessons at school, that number is usually calculated to two decimal places and is commonly recognized as 3.14. But what you might not know is that this number is infinitely long. That is, if you keep on dividing the circumference by the diameter, you get a never-ending number. Pi is sometimes represented as the fraction 22 over 7, which only gives us an approximation of the ratio. This figure has given us in Europe Pi Approximation Day, which is celebrated on the 22nd day of the seventh month, that is July 22nd. However, in the United States World Pi Day is held on March 14th, which in American date notation is written as 3 over 14, representing the first three figures of the decimal representation of pi. Many educational institutions hold special events on these days.

First, I'll talk a little about the significance of pi. Pi has fascinated scholars, mathematicians and scientists for thousands of years and for many, this fascination involves calculating its value with increasing precision. It has numerous practical uses. One of the reasons pi is so well known and studied is that it can be found in so many different formulae. As its ratio relates to circles, it is essential in both trigonometry and geometry and can also be found in dozens of formulae relating to physics, cosmology, electromagnetism, engineering, geology, probability and statistics.

So, let's have a brief look at its history. Well we have to go right back to the Ancient Babylonians to see that some understanding of pi has been around for a long time. As they were building their city, the Ancient Babylonian town planners took a great interest in geometry and as far back as the 20th century BCE, they discovered that if you divide a circle's circumference by its diameter you always get a number in the region of three. Their exact calculation gave this ratio a value of 3.125, which is only half a per cent outside the true value of pi.

We have numerous historical accounts of pi. One of the earliest dates back to the second century BCE and is on an Ancient Egyptian papyrus scroll. This version of pi is in fact a copy of an earlier document and, although not entirely accurate, is within one per cent of its true value at 3.160.

Questions 35–40

35 G

36 C

37 I

38 B

39 A

40 H

Script

Lecturer Over the years numerous notable mathematicians and scientists have worked on defining the value of pi. The famous Greek scholar, Archimedes, working in the first century BCE, took a theoretical approach to the study of pi. He devised a system for working out the value of pi, using polygons, that is a flat shape with at least three sides or angles. This is why it is sometimes called 'Archimedes' constant'. After Archimedes, mathematicians, scientists and astronomers from India, Persia and China attempted to calculate the pi ratio but it wasn't until the 16th and 17th centuries that the development of infinite series techniques allowed far more precise calculations. It was early the following century that a little-known Welsh mathematician by the name of William Jones, a contemporary and friend of Sir Isaac Newton, actually gave the ratio a name, suggesting pi, after the 16th letter of the Greek alphabet.

The 18th and 19th centuries saw two significant breakthroughs for pi. The first was in 1761, when the Swiss mathematician Johann Lambert established that pi is an irrational number. This means that it cannot be expressed as a fraction of two whole numbers. The second breakthrough occurred in 1882 when Ferdinand von Lindemann, a mathematician from Germany, demonstrated that pi was transcendental.

This means that it is not possible to find a square with an exactly equal area to a given circle.

It was another German mathematician, Ludolph van Ceulen who, back at the beginning of the 17th century, calculated pi to 35 decimal places. This achievement really set the ball rolling for the sometimes obsessive quest by mathematicians the world over to find the highest number of digits when calculating pi. Some have devoted years of their lives to this cause, with varying degrees of success. William Shanks, who was not even a professional mathematician, spent around 20 years to calculate pi to 707 decimal places. His achievement was discredited after his death, when it was discovered that he had made a mistake and only the first 527 digits were correct. This error was discovered in 1944 using one of the first digital calculators and the computer era revolutionized mathematicians' ability to find ever-increasing numbers of digits. Throughout the mid-20th century, the record for the number of digits was broken repeatedly until 1973, when over one million digits was reached. Since then the record has gone on to be broken a number of times, many of which used multi-million pound computers. The record is now around 10 trillion digits. That's 10 followed by 12 noughts. One of the most notable achievements was by a Frenchman called Fabrice Bellard, who in 2009 developed a new formula to calculate pi, which has subsequently become known as 'Bellard's formula'. This enabled him to calculate pi to 2,700 billion decimal places. What made his achievement so amazing was that the software programmer used his £2,000 desktop computer, taking 131 days to complete the calculation. His record has since been broken a number of times. Finally, one other notable achievement that might interest you was by a research student, Lu Chao, who in 2005 memorized and recited pi to 67,890 digits, without making a single mistake. The feat took the postgraduate just over 24 hours to complete.

So, as you can see pi is a fascinating number. Moving on now, let's talk a little more about pi's relevance to everyday life ...

Unit 7

Topic talk

1

a bicycles, cars, buses and trains

b–d Students' own answers.

2

a car: drawback

b bike: benefit

c bike/foot (pedestrian): drawback

d car/motorbike: drawback

e bike: drawback

f bike/bus/car: drawback

g bus/train/underground: drawback

h bus/train/underground: benefit

i bike/car/foot (pedestrian): drawback

j car: drawback.

3

a park and ride

b cycle lanes

c pedestrian crossings

d breakdown

e overtake

f congestion

g rush hour

h subsidized

i traffic calming measures

j collision

4

a travel

b journey

c excursion

d location

e upper

f expeditions

g home

h abroad

5

Students' own answers.

6

a negative

b positive

c positive

d negative

e positive

f positive

g positive

h negative

7

Students' own answers.

Listening skills

1

Possible answers

a reading stories, preparing food

b caring for orphaned animals, keeping records of plant/bird species

c transporting materials, painting and decorating

d teaching, playing sports

e giving health advice, talking to families/mothers

f planting trees, gardening

g picking up rubbish from beaches, recording species of seabirds/fish

2

a, b Students' own answers.

c Most would be more likely to be in developing countries.

d as a gap year before going to university, as a sabbatical at any time, after retirement

3

someone doing voluntary work in South America

4

1 a skill or ability

2 a time period

3 an aspect of language learning

4 a person

5 a place

6 a description

7 a place

8 a place or person

5

1 The rubric states answers should be no more than two words.

2 Alternative answers are given; only one is allowed.

3 *words* does not agree with the verb *was* that follows.

4 This repeats the word *his* which is already in the summary.

5 *Peruvian* is an adjective rather than a place.

6 *injured* has exactly the same meaning as the previous word in the summary so is unlikely to be correct.

7 *project* is not a place so unlikely to be correct.

8 *dangerous* is an adjective rather than a noun which is required here following the preposition *from*.

6

1 language skills

2 three months

3 vocabulary

4 flatmates

5 rehabilitation centre

6 orphaned

7 slums

8 the streets

7

See underlined words and phrases in audio script.

Script

Tutor So, Dylan, I see from your personal statement that you've recently spent six months in South America. What made you decide to go there?

Dylan Well, I wanted to do some voluntary work and also improve my language skills. I already speak Spanish – my mother is Colombian. But I wanted to learn some Portuguese too.

Tutor So you spent time in Brazil?

Dylan I enrolled on a 3-month intensive language course in São Paulo. I must say it was difficult learning a language from scratch but it didn't take too long before I could get by pretty well.

Tutor It's like Spanish, isn't it, so that must have helped?

Dylan Yes, a lot of the vocabulary was very familiar to me – some of the words are almost the same as Spanish which made it easy for me but the Brazilians laughed at me because they said I sounded too Spanish, so the pronunciation was a bit of a problem at first. My flatmates were all local students and they really helped me – I picked up a lot from them.

Tutor What was the work you did?

Dylan The main reason I went to Brazil was to take part in a volunteering project on the Amazon.

Tutor That sounds interesting. What exactly were you doing?

Dylan It was in the Peruvian part of the Amazon so my Spanish came in handy. We spent two weeks working at a rehabilitation centre for wild animals which had been brought in injured or orphaned. Most of the time was spent working at the centre helping to feed and care for the animals before they are released back into their natural habitats. We also spent two days trekking in the rain forest with an expert guide helping us spot wildlife and some of the traditional plants they use as medicine.

Tutor That sounds exciting. So what did you do after that?

Dylan I had originally intended to come home at that point but someone I met on the Amazon trip asked me if I had would like to stay on for a couple of months . working at a community day centre for kids on a favela project in Rio de Janeiro.

Tutor Those are the slums aren't they?

Dylan That's right. It was a totally different experience to the Amazon one – really hard work physically and emotionally, but in many ways it was a lot more rewarding.

Tutor Yes, I can imagine. What sort of things were you doing there?

Dylan All sorts of things really. We were responsible for keeping the place clean and cooking but for the most part I was with the children; feeding them, playing with them, teaching them English – anything to keep them out of danger and off the streets – that's the main aim of the centre. I met some amazing people there – both the children and staff and I still keep in touch with some of them. I'm hoping to return next year and spend my summer vacation there, if I can save up enough money.

Tutor Well, good luck with that – it sounds very worthwhile.

Speaking skills

1–4

Students' own answers.

5

The candidate is doing Task A. He would like to visit Malaysia. He would fly there and would visit the capital, the rainforest and the coast. He would like to go because his father lived there as a child and because it is a diverse nation.

Script

I'd like to talk about a country I've always wanted to visit, which is Malaysia. It's a country in south-east Asia and my father lived there when he was young and because he's told me such a lot about it I've always wanted to go to there. One of the things that attracts me is it's such a diverse nation and I think there's something for everyone. There are busy cosmopolitan cities like Kuala Lumpur, there's a beautiful coast, there's rainforest and I think there's plenty to do if you like adventures and sports. If I had the chance to go to this amazing country I'd have to fly there and I'd probably do a tour and visit quite a few different places. My first destination would be the capital. I think it's quite a modern city with lots of new hotels and shopping centres but it also has quite a lot of history and tradition and is very multi-ethnic – you can find Malay, Chinese and Indian influences throughout the city and the effects of colonialism are also evident. I think you can find the mix of cultures in the food too – it's meant to be fantastic and it's not too expensive. Apparently you can get really cheap seafood, which is my favourite, and Malaysian cuisine has a lot of spicy dishes, which I also love. I'd like to go to the rainforest for a few days. I've never been to the jungle before so I think it would be amazing to actually spend a few nights there. I think the journey to get there is quite difficult – you have to go by boat to get to the main settlement and trek on foot if you want to see any wildlife. I expect it's quite hard to see any big animals but you can see a lot of birds and insects and maybe a few monitor lizards if you're lucky. I think I would finish my trip at the seaside, maybe on one of the islands – there's lots of choice I think and the beaches look stunning. I'd like to go to a really quiet one with not too many tourists – I don't like places that are spoilt by too many visitors although it's quite nice to meet a few other travellers. I'd love to snorkel or even learn how to dive but that might not be easy. I think it would be a fantastic holiday and I really hope to be able to go on this trip one day.

6

a nation, country
b city, capital

7

a multi-ethnic; mix of cultures; Malay, Chinese and Indian influences
b seaside, beaches
c jungle
d cuisine, seafood, spicy dishes
e trip, holiday
f animals, birds, insects, monitor lizards
g not too expensive
h hard; not easy
i visitors, travellers

8

Students' own answers.

Pronunciation

1

O	Oo
Spain France Greece	China Poland Norway Russia
oO	**Ooo**
Brazil Japan Iraq Oman	Italy Portugal Germany Mexico
ooO	**oOo**
Vietnam Kazakhstan Pakistan Bangladesh	Morocco Croatia Jamaica

Script

Spain
China
Brazil
Italy
Vietnam
Morocco
Portugal
Croatia
France
Japan
Poland
Germany
Kazakhstan
Jamaica
Greece
Iraq
Oman
Mexico
Pakistan
Norway
Bangladesh
Russia

2

-ish
Spanish Polish
-(i)an
Brazilian Italian Moroccan Croatian German Jamaican Mexican Norwegian Russian
-ese
Chinese Portuguese Japanese Vietnamese
-i
Iraqi Omani Pakistani Bangladeshi
other
French Kazakh Greek

3

The stress usually falls on the syllable before the ending, so if the adjective ends in -ish, the stress will fall on the syllable before, if the adjective ends in -ian, the stress comes on the preceding syllable. The exception is adjectives ending in -ese, where the stress falls on the final syllable.

Script

Spanish
Chinese
Brazilian
Italian
Vietnamese
Moroccan
Portuguese
Croatian
French
Japanese
Polish
German
Kazakh
Jamaican
Greek
Iraqi
Omani
Mexican
Pakistani
Norwegian
Bangladeshi
Russian

4

Possible answers

Swedish, Malaysian, Sudanese, Saudi, Czech

5

All are languages apart from: Brazilian (Portuguese), Moroccan (Arabic/French), Jamaican (English), Mexican (Spanish), Iraqi (Arabic/Kurdish), Omani (Arabic), Pakistani (Urdu and others), Bangladesh (Bengali and others).

6

1 Italian
2 Portuguese
3 Japan
4 Spanish
5 Greek
6 Japanese
7 Russian
8 Iraq
9 Norwegian
10 French
11 Russia
12 Germany

7

Students' own answers.

Exam listening

Questions 21–24

21 C
22 B
23 B
24 A

Script

Carlos Hi Shereen. How's it going?

Shereen Oh, Hello Carlos. I'm OK, I suppose, but it's just that I've got so much work to do and this morning my tutor set another project and I've no idea what to do for this one.

Carlos What's it about?

Shereen Well, we have to choose a topic but it's got to be related to transport in some way. I honestly have no idea. I was just going to the library to get some ideas.

Carlos I don't know if this will be any help but I saw a TV programme last week about traffic problems – it was really interesting – you may be able to still catch it online.

Shereen What was so interesting?

Carlos Well, a lot of it was looking at congestion in different countries – I didn't realize it was so bad. Did you know that there are around 800 million vehicles in the world – I think that's what they said – and this figure is growing all the time by about 50 million every year apparently.

Shereen That's amazing! What's going to happen to them all?

Carlos Good question. I think they said the number would double in the next two decades. And of course all that traffic causes congestion, which costs the economy millions. I think they said that in the US it costs the economy $100 billion every year.

Shereen Well, they do drive a lot of cars.

Carlos Yes, but it's happening all over the world. In Moscow they lose around $12 billion a year and of course nations like China and India are growing all the time. More cars mean more time wasted sitting in traffic jams.

Shereen So what's the solution?

Carlos Well, there's been a great deal of research into the whole congestion problem and numerous solutions have been put forward. For instance, in some Chinese cities they restrict road use by banning certain motorists from driving one day a week, depending on their car registration number and you know about the congestion charge in London, where you have to pay to drive in certain parts of the city.

Shereen Yes, but these don't really solve anything, do they, and they probably just get people more frustrated. I know I'd get annoyed if I couldn't drive in to the city on certain days or had to pay.

Carlos Well, one of interesting things they talked about on the programme was why we get traffic jams in the first place.

Shereen Surely it's just weight of traffic?

Carlos Well, yes, but you know sometimes you're driving along on the motorway and the traffic seems to be flowing freely when all of a sudden, there's a traffic jam.

Shereen Yes, I always assumed it was due to an accident or a breakdown.

Carlos Not necessarily. Scientists have been looking at this for years and have used all sort of computer simulators to recreate the situation on the road. Until recently they thought the same as you, that congestion was caused by sheer weight of traffic. But they have now discovered that it's also due to driver action.

Shereen Do you mean bad driving?

Carlos No, it's more to do with unpredictable actions. Suppose a lorry suddenly changes lanes or something else happens that you're not expecting, well, this can have an enormous effect apparently.

Shereen How exactly?

Carlos Well, what they discovered was that under certain conditions, if just one driver overreacts to an event like that, by braking too hard suddenly, this can then set off a reaction that will send shockwaves for miles back down the motorway

Shereen How come?

Carlos Well, when the first car brakes, the car behind has to brake too and so on until the cars start to gather in clumps. That's how you get those stop-start congestion waves, which can eventually result in gridlock when all the traffic comes to a standstill.

Shereen And is it only motorways that are affected?

Carlos No, any road junction where two or more lanes of traffic join together can cause problems. For example, as vehicles join a motorway they tend to cut across lanes, which causes other cars to slow down or brake. This can affect vehicles miles behind on the motorway.

Questions 25–30

25 real time
26 speed limits
27 2,000
28 some sections
29 radar
30 braking

Script

Shereen So is there anything that can be done about it?

Carlos Well, one measure that has been introduced is on the M25 motorway, which goes round London. They've set up a system whereby experts use real time data collected from monitors on the motorway and analyse it in order to set speed limits.

Shereen So they're looking at live action on the motorway?

Carlos Exactly. Because they're working in real time and reacting immediately to the situation on the road, they hope to alleviate problems before they happen. So as the traffic gets heavier to the point where these waves of congestion are likely to form, the controllers monitoring the situation set speed limits at say, 50 or 60 mph to regulate the flow. Further back down the motorway at the back of the congestion zone, they set a lower speed limit, say 40 mph, which should theoretically help control the traffic through the problem area.

Shereen But traffic jams still happen on the M25, don't they? I was in one a few months ago and we were at a standstill for ages.

Carlos Yes, of course, sometimes there are simply too many cars on the roads. I think what the programme said was that the ideal number of cars on the road is no more than 2,000 per lane per hour – something like that. Theoretically, this should keep traffic moving smoothly at all times. But of course the number of cars on the road far exceeds this – I think there are some sections of the M25 which have up to 200,000 vehicles a day.

Shereen Mmm. So, basically we need to reduce the number of cars on the roads. Well, that's not likely to happen, is it?

Carlos No, but researchers are still looking into car technology that might help. As most congestion waves are caused by drivers braking too hard suddenly, the idea is that you install radar on the outside of the car and an on-board computer. The driver would activate the system when signs alerted him or her to a possible congestion zone. Then the computer would take over and then take control of the braking and acceleration. Because it can react much faster than a human driver, in theory, it would control the car smoothly through the zone.

Shereen A bit like an auto-pilot system?

Carlos Yes.

Shereen Well, it does sound interesting. Do you think I could do something with this for my project?

Carlos Why don't we have a look to see if we can find the programme online? That should get you started.

Unit 8

Topic talk

1

Students' own answers.

2

1 e
2 f
3 h
4 i
5 j
6 c
7 b
8 g
9 d
10 a

3

Students' own answers.

4

a up; up to
b back; back on
c after; on
d down; out
e away; over
f up to; apart
g up; up with

5

a dull
b changeable
c selfish
d serious
e cynical
f lazy
g reserved
h aggressive

6, 7

Students' own answers.

Listening skills

1

1 C
2 A
3 A
4 B
5 C
6 A
7 B
8 B
9 A
10 C

Script

1 The reference number is GI435AIH.
2 The address is 14 Wainwright Road.
3 The postcode is CV13 6JG.
4 The Flight number is EH 6358.
5 The credit card number is 6595 4420 8569 5855.
6 His surname is Lindsay – that's L-I-N-D-S-A-Y.
7 Her passport number is 935465006.
8 The telephone number is 07448356483.
9 The email address is williams14@mail.com, that's W-I-L-L-I-A-M-S-1-4- @ mail.com.
10 The room number is B938.

2

1 a surname
2 the name of a street
3 a telephone number
4 a date or time
5 a time or place
6 a date or time
7 a time or place
8 a reference
9 a noun
10 a reference

3

1 Chamberlain
2 Market Street
3 07934 854552
4 Saturday
5 8.45 am
6 Monday 27th April
7 5 pm
8 CHAMB 703161 SW LY 60
9 car seat
10 B657D64

Script

Assistant Good morning. Abbey Car Hire. How can I help you?

Customer Oh hello. I'm calling to see if it's possible to hire a car for three days next weekend.

Assistant What size of car were you hoping to rent?

Customer Well, something big enough for a family of four with luggage.

Assistant That would be a medium family car. Let's see … yes, that shouldn't be a problem – there's plenty of availability. First I need to take a few details. Can I have your name please?

Customer Yes, it's Steven with a V, Chamberlain, that's C-H-A-M-B-E-R-L-A-I-N.

Assistant OK, and can I have your address, please?

Customer Yes, it's 3 Hamilton House.

Assistant Oh, that's in Queens Road, isn't it?

Customer No, we don't live in Rowington, we're from Stretton. It must be a different Hamilton House – it's Market Street, Stretton.

Assistant And the postcode?

Customer ST17 5BU

Assistant And a contact telephone number. Your mobile is probably best.

Customer Yes, let's see, it's 07934 854552.

Assistant So, can you confirm the exact dates you wish to hire the car. From Friday you said?

Customer No, Saturday morning if possible. That's the 25th. What's the earliest we can pick it up?

Assistant Our office opens at 8 am.

Customer Oh, not that early – I expect about a quarter to nine would suit us.

Assistant OK, 8.45 on the Saturday. And you'll drop it off on the Monday?

Customer Yes, April 27th – that's right. We have a train to catch at half past six so we'd like to drop it off in the afternoon at about half four?

Assistant Actually we offer a complimentary shuttle service to the station and airport. If your train's at 6.30, may I suggest a 5 o'clock drop off? That will give you plenty of time – the shuttle bus takes no more than 20 minutes, even in the rush hour.

Customer That's great – thanks, that'll save us a taxi fare.

Assistant So, the total charge will be, let's see … £87.50. That includes full insurance.

Customer That seems reasonable.

Assistant I just need a few more details. Who is going to be the main driver?

Customer I am.

Assistant You'll just need to bring your driving licence with you. You haven't got the number on you have you?

Customer Yes, wait a minute. Yes, here it is, it's CHAMB 703161 SW LY 60.

Assistant And will you be the only driver?

Customer Yes, my wife prefers not to drive when we hire a car. I've just remembered – we'll need a car seat for my youngest son. Is that possible?

Assistant How old is he?

Customer Four.

Assistant Yes, that's fine. I've added that to the booking form – there'll be a charge of £10 for the car seat. So that's everything. I'll just give you the booking reference number – it's B657D64.

Customer Got that.

Answer Key

Assistant We'll send you a confirmation email with all the details.
Customer Thank you.
Assistant You're welcome. Thank you Mr Chamberlain.

Speaking skills

1

Candidate B gives the better response. Candidate A uses quite a lot of repetition, whilst Candidate B uses a wider range of language and other techniques to avoid repetition.

2

Candidate B No I don't think <u>so</u> (it's important for friends to have similar personalities). It would be very boring and predictable if friends all had the same <u>character</u> (personality). I think sometimes the most interesting relationships are <u>the ones</u> (the relationships) between very different <u>individuals</u> (personalities). People sometimes assume that <u>this</u> <u>type of friendship</u> (relationships between different personalities) can lead to arguments but they don't <u>have to</u> (have to lead to arguments). For example, one person could be quite sociable whilst <u>her</u> (the person's) friend <u>isn't</u> (isn't sociable), but together <u>their</u> (the two friends') personalities can make a good balance.

3

Reference: this (type), her (friend), their (personalities)
Lexical cohesion: character (personality), individuals (personalities)
Substitution: so (that it's important), the ones (the relationships)
Ellipsis: have to (lead to arguments), isn't (sociable)

4

1 b
2 e
3 a
4 c
5 g
6 f
7 h
8 d

5

1b One of the main duties of parents: Another one (substitution)
their children: them (reference)
2e not affected his ability to be successful in life: Neither has (substitution)
3a has increased significantly: This rise (reference and lexical cohesion)
older people: the elderly (lexical cohesion)

4c Growing up bilingual: it (reference)
children: their (reference)
5g should try to have a positive and optimistic outlook on life: Doing so (substitution)
6f serious consequences: These (reference)
young children: their (reference)
7h it is important to give money to help poor people overseas: such a view (lexical cohesion)
8d My grandparents: they (reference)
had a great influence on me: do so (substitution)

6

a Do parents read to their children as much as they should ~~read to their children~~?
b Should couples who have children be given more financial benefits than couples who don't ~~have children~~?
c Do you think that couples who share the housework equally are likely to have fewer arguments than couples who don't ~~share the housework equally~~?
d Do you help around the house as much as you could ~~help around the house~~?
e Do young children who go to nursery have more opportunities for social interaction than children who don't ~~go to nursery~~?
f Do you think men tend to help more around the home than they used to ~~help around the home~~?

7

Students' own answers.

Pronunciation

1

a my friends are
b others haven't
c to do so
d it is
e I would
f would like to
g I was
h I wouldn't

2

The auxiliary verbs are all stressed to contrast with the previous verb and come at the end of the sentence (no weak forms at the end of a sentence).

Script

a Some teenagers in my school are not very well-behaved but fortunately all my friends are.
b I've had a very happy childhood so I sometimes forget that others haven't.
c Spending quality time together is important for most families but unfortunately it's not always possible to do so.
d Some people think that having a child is not a major responsibility but obviously it is.
e My parents didn't have a good education so they were determined that I would.
f Not everyone wants to keep in touch with their old school friends when they leave school but I would like to.
g I would like to bring up my children in a large family just as I was.
h Many of my friends say they want to leave home to study overseas but I wouldn't.

3

Student's own answers.

4

See words and phrases in audio script. Weak forms are <u>underlined</u>, strong forms are **bold**.

5

Students' own answers.

Script

a I'd like <u>to</u> leave home one day but I'm not sure if I'm ready **to** yet.
b I'm lucky – I<u>'ve</u> had far better opportunities in life than my parents **did**.
c I thought young children <u>could</u> be difficult but teenagers **can** too!
d Couples who **don't** have much money often wait until they **do** before having children.
e I loved being part of a big family when I <u>was</u> young and I still **do**.
f Being shy <u>has</u> never <u>been</u> a disadvantage <u>for</u> me, but I know it **can be** <u>for</u> some.
g When I <u>was</u> young I would <u>have</u> loved <u>to</u> have an older brother <u>to</u> look up **to**.
h Children today <u>are</u> sometimes more confident about using technology than their parents and teachers **are**.

109

Exam listening

Questions 1–3

1 C
2 B
3 A

Script

Alan Look Caroline. I picked up this leaflet in the library today. It's about a family arts festival they're holding in Eastfield in July. It looks really good.

Caroline Oh, that must be the thing Jane was telling me about – it takes place every other year apparently and it attracts thousands of people from the local area – she said it's really worth going to.

Alan Yes, this must be it. Look, there's loads of different things on.

Caroline Let's see – lots of different types of music, dance, comedy, theatre, cinema – whatever you fancy really – yes you're right, there's a huge variety.

Alan Do you think there's enough to keep the kids happy?

Caroline Well it's supposed to be a family festival. Look there's storytelling for kids, circus skills, puppet shows, all sorts of things for them.

Alan So, what do you think? Shall we all go and take the kids?

Caroline I think it's a great idea. How much are the tickets?

Alan Well, I don't think you can get an all-inclusive ticket – it says here you pay separately for each different event you choose to go to, but it advises you to book in advance for the most popular shows like the headline music acts. You can't just turn up and get tickets on the day.

Caroline So, we need to have a look at the programme and decide which ones to book.

Questions 4–10

4 awh1163
5 07894 734556
6 6/six weeks
7 folk
8 Theatre Society
9 1/one adult
10 £3.50

Script

Caroline OK, so I've got the booking form. Shall I put your name down?

Alan Yes, that's probably easier.

Caroline OK, so, Name: Alan Hardy. I can never remember your email address.

Alan It's awh1163@mailgroup.com

Caroline A-W-H-1-6-3

Alan 1-1-6-3.

Caroline 1-1-6-3@mailgroup.com. And which telephone number shall I put down?

Alan My mobile is probably better – you can't remember that either can you? It's 07894 734556. Don't they want our address?

Caroline No, I think it's all done electronically, which is good.

Alan What about the tickets? Do we pick them up on the door?

Caroline No, it says here that they'll email the tickets six weeks before the event.

Alan Which events do you fancy going to?

Caroline Well, I must say it's quite hard to choose but something I definitely want to see is the folk group The Stags.

Alan Yes, they're the headline act on the first night. What do you know about them?

Caroline Well, they're a big group, 11 or 12 members, and they do a mixture of traditional and modern folk music. They play lots of different instruments – they're supposed to be fantastic live and it's suitable for kids too. The tickets are £8.50 but I think there are reductions for children.

Alan So, I'll put down for four tickets for all of us, 2 adults, 2 children. What else?

Caroline Well, I thought the production of Robin Hood on the Saturday afternoon might be worth going to. It's by the Eastfield Theatre Society and I've heard they're very good.

Alan But that clashes with Gordon Hayburn – I really wanted to see him.

Caroline Oh, he's that singer songwriter you like, isn't he?

Alan Yes – I'm really keen to see him – he's fantastic.

Caroline I'll tell you what – I'll take the children to see Robin Hood and you can go to see Gordon.

Alan Are you sure?

Caroline Yes, I'm not too keen on his style of music and the children would enjoy the play.

Alan So I'll put down 1 adult and 2 kids for Robin Hood. The tickets are only £5 for that. And we'll have one ticket for Gordon. He's a bit more – £7.50 each but he's worth it. I've been wanting to see him live for ages.

Caroline Great. What about the Sunday? I think it might be nice to see the Irish Drumming group, Crash.

Alan Yes, they look good but I don't think I can book anything for Sunday. It's my mum's birthday remember and I should really spend the day with her.

Caroline Do you mind if I get tickets for me and the kids?

Alan Not at all – go ahead. I'll put all three of you down. The tickets are only £3.50 – that sounds like good value

Caroline It's a shame we can't go to more events but I'm sure there'll be lots of other things on at the venues.

Alan Yes. Well, I'll get this sent off today, shall I?

Unit 9

Topic talk

1

1 a If you have money, it will serve you well, but if you owe money, it will control you.
  b To get money, you have to work hard.
  c It is easy to lose all your money if you don't behave sensibly.
  d The most valuable things in life (love, good health) do not have to be paid for.

2, 3 Students' own answers.

2

1 expense
2 deposit
3 be in debt
4 save
5 pay for
6 pocket money.
7 been left
8 income
9 cut back
10 expenditure

3

1 outgoing
2 savings
3 owe
4 invest
5 afford
6 allowance
7 inherited
8 salary
9 economize
10 spending

4

a 5
b 10
c 1
d 9
e 6
f 8
g 2
h 3
i 7
j 4

5, 6

Students' own answers.

7

a priceless
b well off
c costly
d discounted
e extravagant
f off-the-shelf
g designer

8

Students' own answers.

Listening skills

1

Students' own answers.

2

a coins (the British 50 pence piece)
b Students' own answers.
c 1 a feature of the coin
  2 something the coin is used in
  3 possibly a metal
  4 a measurement
  5 a date
  6 a feature on the face of the coin

3

1 curved sides
2 vending machines
3 75% copper
4 27.5 mm
5 1998
6 seated figure

Script

As you can see, the coin is heptagonal in shape – that means it's seven-sided. The shape could be problematic as most coins are round so that they can be easily used in vending machines. The 50 pence piece however has been designed with curved sides and as you can see, the edges are rounded off so that it'll still function in vending machines. This also gives it its constant diameter. Like most silver-coloured coins nowadays, it's made from an alloy called cupronickel – that's 75% copper and 25% nickel. Over the years the coin has changed in weight and dimension and now weighs only 8 grams but it started life a lot heavier at 13.5 grams. It has also shrunk slightly in size and is now 27.5 millimetres in diameter, that's 2.5 millimetres less than it used to be. The obverse of the coin, or face, shows a portrait of Her Majesty Queen Elizabeth the Second and there have been three different portraits used over the years. The current one first appeared in 1998 and is a much more realistic version than the previous two. The reverse was originally intended to be the Royal Arms but was replaced at the last minute by the distinctive design of the seated figure of Britannia, the Roman name for Britain, which is today used as a female personification of the island.

4

1 A agrees and B disagrees.
2 A disagrees and B agrees.
3 A agrees and B disagrees.
4 A disagrees and B agrees.
5 A agrees and B disagrees.

Script

1 I think people can lead a happy life without money.
  A Well it's certainly not impossible.
  B Of course they can't!
2 I think all pop stars earn far too much money.
  A Surely that's a slight exaggeration?
  B Don't they just!
3 Rich people just don't understand the true value of money.
  A I couldn't agree with you more.
  B I'm not sure that's a fair assessment.
4 I don't believe saving money is relevant in today's society.
  A It's never been more relevant.
  B Well, you have a point there.
5 Footballers deserve more money.
  A Oh, absolutely!
  B You're not serious!

5

Agreement
It's certainly not impossible
Don't they just!
I couldn't agree with you more.
Well, you have a point there.
Oh, absolutely!

Disagreement
Of course they can't!
Surely that's a slight exaggeration?
I'm not sure that's a fair assessment.
It's never been more relevant.
You're not serious!

6

a P
b P (Anne appears to agree but her tone is sarcastic)
c B
d P
e A
f A

Script

Anne I've just heard an interview on the radio in which they were discussing student loans – apparently more and more students are now getting into debt and it's taking some of them years to pay it off.
Paul Yes, I read something about that in the newspaper yesterday. It said that unless graduates can find extremely well-paid jobs, they are finding it difficult to pay back their loans.
Anne What I don't understand is why some students get into so much debt in the first place. Apparently, some students owe more than £50,000 by the time they graduate; that seems excessive to me.
Paul Not when you consider the cost of fees, books, accommodation and the general cost of living – it all adds up. It's only to be expected really.
Anne But surely they should take measures to make sure they don't end up with so much debt, like taking a part-time job for instance? They said on the radio that under a third of students have part-time work.
Paul Well, I imagine it's not easy to find a job and you've got to fit it in with your studies – they probably don't have time.
Anne Oh, yes, and all students study so hard and have absolutely no free time to do anything else!
Paul Jobs suitable for students aren't always easy to come by though and don't forget they're not that well paid anyway.

Anne Well, you could be right there – my friend Miriam was paid next to nothing for the cleaning job she had. Well, if it were me, I'd ask my parents to lend me the money, then I wouldn't have to worry about high interest rates and could pay the money back at my leisure.

Paul Do you think everyone has parents who can afford to do that? Mine would certainly struggle. And most students would rather be independent; they don't want to have to rely on or be indebted to their parents for years.

Anne I'd still rather owe my family than owe a bank. Well, I think the only way to avoid the situation is to not bother with university and try to start earning as soon as you leave school.

Paul Isn't that a bit of a drastic solution? What if you couldn't find a job? Some jobs have thousands of applicants nowadays – with a degree under your belt, surely you're more likely to find a good job?

Anne But even for graduate jobs there's tremendous competition. I'm not sure it's a guarantee of getting work anymore and certainly not a job that's going to pay off your loans! You could just end up with mountains of debt and no job at the end of it all!

Paul We seem to have come full circle here. Let's continue this over a coffee.

Anne Good idea! Um, who's paying?

Speaking skills

1
A an item of technology
B a piece of jewellery
C a piece of furniture

2

	A	B	C
General description	the latest model	a family heirloom	decorative and useful
Where they got it	online	from great-grandmother	an old junk shop
Appearance	tiny slim and streamlined silver	not in perfect condition the gold has a few scratches	looks as if it's got an interesting history marks on wood hand-painted drawer knobs
What it's used for	can do many things	worn for special family occasions	DVD storage
What it means to the speaker	likes the design couldn't live without it	of great sentimental value means a great deal to her	immediately appealed to him/her really fond of it

3, 4
Students' own answers.

5
It is discussing something you bought rather than a possession (which could have been a gift or inherited). It requires you to talk about the process of saving for the item and why you wanted to buy it rather than what it means to you.

6
Students' own answers.

7
1 c
2 d
3 b
4 a

8
Students' own answers.

Pronunciation

1
a noun
b noun
c noun
d verb
e verb
f verb
g verb
h noun

2
O o: a, b, c, h
o O: d, e, f, g
For the nouns the stress is on the first syllable; for the verbs it is on the second.

Script

a If the goods are faulty we will give a full refund.
b I like shopping for fresh produce in local farmers' markets.
c I don't like giving money as a present – it doesn't seem very personal.
d Interest rates are set to increase again next month.
e I took it back to the shop but they wouldn't refund the money.
f I wasn't sure when to present him with the bill for my work.
g I don't know how that shop manages to produce such inexpensive clothing.
h The recent increase in the cost of living has made life very difficult for many families.

3
Students' own answers.

4
a noun; noun
b noun; noun
c verb; verb
d noun; verb
e noun; verb
f verb; noun
g verb; noun
h verb; noun

5, 6
The verbs follow the stress pattern o O; the nouns O o.

Script

a If you bought something which had a defect, would you take it back and ask for a refund?

b Has there been an increase in the cost of public transport in your town recently?

c Would you object to paying higher taxes if public services were increased?

d Do you prefer to buy fresh produce locally or fruit and vegetables imported from other countries?

e Do you always take a present when you're invited to someone's house?

f Would you refuse to work if your employer tried to change your contract or working conditions?

g Should the public be permitted to read a company's financial records or should they be kept private?

h Do you think that students have a right to protest about increases in fees?

7
Students' own answers.

Exam listening

Questions 21–4

21 B
22 A
23 A
24 B

Script

Isabelle So, Rob, what do you think about your essay title?

Rob 'Money is not the only measure of success in life' ... Mmm, I don't feel very inspired somehow. I'm struggling with ideas at the moment. What do you think, Ed?

Ed Well, there's certainly plenty you can say on the topic but it's evidence and examples to back up your argument that they're looking for – have you got any?

Isabelle I'm sure there must be plenty – even from your own life experiences. You must know some successful people who aren't necessarily wealthy, Rob?

Rob I suppose so. I mean, you can be successful but that doesn't always mean you are fantastically paid. Take nurses, for example – they aren't paid well but do a very worthwhile job. You can't say they're not successful, can you?

Ed That's true. But with many jobs good pay does equal success – most top businessmen and bankers get really high salaries and what about top sportsmen and women? Some footballers earn a fortune.

Rob Yes, but that doesn't mean success always equals money. There are plenty of examples to disprove that claim, I think.

Isabelle Yes, what about all the people who do things for no pay at all – volunteers and people who do things for charity? A friend of my mother's has been volunteering at a local youth group for years. She works full-time too but isn't well-off and she puts in hours of her free time every week. I would definitely say she's a success. I think you should be able to measure someone's success by what they give back to society.

Ed I don't think it's the only way to be successful though. There are different types of success I suppose. Material success is certainly one of the most obvious tangible ways of judging success. If someone owns a big house and drives a fast car, you automatically assume they're successful.

Rob But they might not have earned that money. It could be inherited or won in the lottery.

Isabelle Or stolen!

Rob Exactly! Not all rich people have earned or even deserve their wealth so can you say they're successful?

Ed What about stars and singers then? Most of them are rich and successful.

Isabelle And all extremely talented! Mmm. Some famous people just rely on good looks or luck to get them where they are. And there are some very gifted actors who never get to Hollywood and make millions of dollars. Does that mean they're not successful?

Ed I think we're forgetting something important. What about academic achievement and success? That's got nothing to do with wealth.

Isabelle But it has – if you do well at school and university, you're more likely to go on to get a well-paid job later in life.

Ed Yes, but my point is that you can be a success at a young age through what you do at school. And, although that may have a bearing on what happens later in your life, at that stage it's not about money, is it?

Isabelle I suppose not. And nowadays academic achievement is no guarantee to finding a good job anyway – so many graduates seem to struggle to find work. And not everyone studies in order to improve their career chances. Some people just do it for pleasure.

Rob Absolutely – or to add to their skills and knowledge and improve themselves as individuals. It's true not everyone

views academic study as a pathway to a money-making career. I have a friend who's recently finished a Master's degree and now wants to do a PhD and for him, it's all about his passion for his subject. I don't think he's even thought about what he'll do at the end of it all.

Ed And it's not just academic success either. There are all sorts of other things you can be successful at that don't necessarily bring you wealth. What about sporting achievements and music?

Isabelle Mm, and success in your personal life – your family – that's so important to many people. You know what they say: money can't bring you happiness. I know lots of people who would rather be in a happy, fulfilling relationship than be rolling in money.

Ed I'd like both!

Isabelle Well, ideally I suppose most people would. But seriously, there's enough evidence to prove the theory wrong, don't you think?

Questions 25–30

25 peace of mind
26 feeling valued
27 freedom to choose
28 67%
29 sports and hobbies
30 58%

Script

Isabelle So, how are you getting on with your essay Rob?

Rob Really well, actually. I've almost finished and I'm quite pleased with it. I just need to write the conclusion and tidy things up a bit.

Isabelle Great! So you found enough to talk about then?

Rob Too much really. I found quite a few articles that really helped me and I even found a national survey which was carried out last year to see what ordinary people think about success. I've included some of the results in my survey. It's quite interesting really – have a look.

Isabelle Oh, do you mean this chart?

Rob Yes. The people in the survey were asked to rank the things they considered to be the most important indicators of success for them and as you can see it seems that, in general, most people are more concerned with other things than possessions and riches. You can see that by far the most popular factor was a happy family life.

Isabelle 82%. Yes, that is high. What came next?

Rob I was quite surprised but health and peace of mind was quite close behind. I hadn't really considered that to be a factor in personal success.

Isabelle I don't think it's that surprising when you think about it. Particularly as you get older, you have more responsibilities and worries about jobs, health and family. Even if you're successful it's difficult to appreciate it if you're in poor health or are constantly stressed or worried about something.

Rob Job satisfaction comes quite high – 73%. Well, that's no surprise – it's great if you love your job and find it rewarding. I can't imagine feeling a success if you hate what you do. And after that came, feeling valued. That's an interesting one.

Isabelle Is that at work?

Rob Both work and home, I think.

Isabelle I can understand that; it's always good to feel appreciated for something you've done and share your successes. What's the first thing you do as a child when you get a good mark or achieve something at school?

Rob Run home and tell your parents! Yes, I agree, being praised and respected for what you do, whether it's by family, friends, colleagues or your boss, is always a good feeling. Next on the list has a score of 69%: freedom to choose.

Isabelle What does that mean exactly?

Rob I think it's to do with having freedom to be able to decide what you do with your life, to choose whether to work from home, or be self-employed. Whether to work long hours or take a day off work. I suppose the more successful you are, the more freedom you're likely to have.

Isabelle I can see that owning your own home, car and other possessions does come quite high – 67% – but not as high as I thought it might. I expected it to be in the eighties or nineties! But that means 33% of people don't consider material wealth to be an important sign of success.

Rob I think it's interesting that even things like achievements outside work were quite close behind – 62% said these were important.

Isabelle Is that things like sports and hobbies?

Rob Yes, well, we talked about that, didn't we? I think doing something like singing in a concert or running in a marathon can give someone a great sense of personal achievement.

Isabelle I'm surprised that the last one doesn't get a higher score; academic and professional qualifications and achievements. I would have thought that these are important to people but only 58% seem to agree – that's more than 40% who don't seem to consider success in education and work important. I wonder why.

Rob Maybe they become less important as you get older and not everyone is concerned with academic success. Remember this survey spoke to a cross-section of society – people of all ages and backgrounds.

Isabelle Well, these survey results will have made your essay interesting. Well done for finding them.

Rob Thanks.

Unit 10

Topic talk

1
Students' own answers.

2
a spend/waste
b allow
c reduce
d devote
e waste/spend
f find
g have
h save

3
Students' own answers.

4
a preceding
b antique
c old
d Present
e Rising
f elderly
g New; old

5
Students' own answers.

6
a past
b future
c present
d present and future
e past and present
f past and present
g future
h future
i past, present and future

7
a a short time ago; used to
b sure; sooner or later
c are inclined; nowadays
d practise
e Seldom
f since I started school
g forecast; in the next ten years
h don't anticipate; near future
i plan; when

8, 9
Students' own ideas.

Listening skills

1
Students' own ideas.

2
Correct order: c, f, a, g, e, h, d, b.

Script

Let me begin by outlining the main areas of my talk today. Firstly, I'll briefly discuss how poor time management can affect us in the workplace and at home. Then we'll consider the implications of poor time management in a little more detail by considering a specific case study. Finally, we'll look at some simple techniques that I hope will help you organize your time more effectively, before question time. By the way, there are leaflets being passed round with details of these strategies – please take a copy away with you. In addition, I have a number of information packs and posters which you're welcome to take if you're interested. So as I was saying, there will be a chance at the end of my talk for any questions you might have. So turning now to the first part of my talk – poor time management.

3, 4

Starting
Let me begin by; I'll start by
Adding
In addition; furthermore
Sequencing
Firstly, then, finally; lastly; after that; next; secondly
Changing topic
turning now to; having talked about X, let's now ...; moving on to; let's now consider
Digressing (going off the topic)
By the way; incidentally
Returning to the topic
as I was saying; returning to my main point
Concluding
(no example in 2) to sum up; to conclude

5

a The process of receiving and dealing with emails.
b 1 an adjective (importance of email)
   2 a verb (action to describe something done to emails)
   3 a noun or noun phrase (to describe the inbox)
   4 a noun or verb (action to be taken if email is not important)
   5 a noun or verb (action to be taken if email is important)
   6 a noun or verb (to refer to the action of filing)
   7 a noun, verb or adjective (to describe a file or action to be taken with a file)
   8 a noun or verb (action to be taken if email can be dealt with quickly)
   9 a noun (a person)
   10 a noun (refers to a plan to be made)
c Students' own answers.

6

1 not urgent
2 reduce
3 significant proportion

Script

Let's now consider what you should do when a new email arrives in your inbox at work. It's useful to know that like all tasks, emails can be classified into four groups depending on their importance and the urgency with which they need to be dealt. Remember that an important email may not be urgent enough to be dealt with immediately. Similarly, an email which needs to be dealt with promptly might not be particularly important. There are of course emails that are important and require immediate attention but, by managing your inbox effectively you should be able to reduce the number of these significantly. The final group is the emails that are neither important nor urgent, which can account for a significant proportion of your inbox.

7

4 delete (the email)
5 further action
6 future reference
7 pending (work)
8 do it now
9 junior colleague
10 clear deadline

Script

The first thing you need to consider when a new email arrives is whether the email is important or not. You may be surprised that around half of all emails we receive have no importance and require no further action. If this is the case, than it is safe to delete the email.

However, if you have decided that yes, the email is important, then several outcomes are possible. The next question to ask yourself is, does the email require further action? Some important emails may not need a response so you may decide that, whilst it contains important information, no further action is necessary. In this case, the email should be filed in a folder for future reference only.

Having decided that the email does require attention, it is now that you need to consider the urgency of the response. If you deem the email to be non-urgent it should be placed in a folder for pending work, that is awaiting attention in the short term.

However, if it requires prompt attention, you now need to consider how long the task will take. If it is something that will take a matter of minutes, then of course the simple solution is to do it now. It could be just a simple matter of sending off a quick reply to the email. That'll be one more thing ticked off your to-do list. However, if it is a task that requires more time, you need to ask yourself if you're the only person capable of accomplishing the task. If the answer is no, then see if there is a junior colleague to whom you can delegate some or all of the task. If you decide the job must be completed by you alone, then this is where you start planning your course of action. This should include making a note in your diary or organizer and giving yourself a clear deadline for the task completion. It might also involve making appointments, arranging meetings and so on.

So, to sum up, managing your inbox does require some thought and effort but believe me, it's well worth it.

Speaking skills

1
a tourism
b food and diet
c shopping; advertising
d children and young people
e sport; global understanding
f TV; children
g leisure
h work
i travel; the future
j transport; the environment

2
1 h
2 b
3 j
4 c

Script

1 It **certainly** shows loyalty to the company but I think most employers prefer it if their workers have broad experience in different work contexts. **There's not the slightest chance** of promotion if you don't have this experience and, professionally, I don't think it's very fulfilling. Personally, if I had the opportunity, I would try to get as much different experience as possible. **It's bound to** make you more employable.

2 **There's a good likelihood** that our lives will become busier so I imagine fast, convenient foods will be even more popular. But I think if that happens, there will be a greater emphasis on healthy fast food so **it may well be** that you will find more restaurants serving quality takeaway meals, not just hamburgers and pizzas. I also think **it's quite likely** that more unusual foods and foods from different countries will become more readily available.

3 This is already quite a serious situation and if we didn't have a great park and ride scheme in the city, it would be even worse. It won't get any better unless serious measures are taken. The trouble is, even if you provide better and cheaper public transport, people will still prefer the convenience of using their own private car and **it's highly unlikely** that making bus fares cheaper will change their minds.

4 Much more than I think most people realize. **It's quite possible** that there are products I wouldn't have bought if I hadn't seen an advert for them. Advertising is all around us, even when we're not really aware of it. **I doubt whether** there is anyone who has not been affected by advertising, even if it is only subconsciously.

3
a prefer; have
b had; would try
c 's; don't have
d happens; will be
e didn't have; would be
f won't get; unless
g even if; will still prefer
h wouldn't have bought; hadn't seen

4

	Past	Present/ Future
Possible		a, c, d, f, g
Hypothetical	h	b, e

5
Certain: certainly; It's bound to
Probable: There's a good likelihood; It may well be; It's quite likely
Possible: It's quite possible
Improbable: I doubt whether; It's highly unlikely
Impossible: There's not the slightest chance

6, 7
Students' own ideas.

Pronunciation

1
a, b   best-selling
c, d   far-reaching

2
See underlined words in audio script.

Script
a Her books on time travel have been best-<u>selling</u>.
b She's written a number of <u>best</u>-selling books on time travel.
c The effects of postponing the election will be far-<u>reaching</u>.
d The postponement of the election will have <u>far</u>-reaching effects.
3 When the adjective is followed by a noun, the stress falls on the first word. When the adjective is used without a noun the stress falls on the second word.

4, 5
See underlined words in audio script.

Script
a What are the benefits and drawbacks of buying <u>mass</u>-produced goods? What about products that are custom-<u>made</u>?
b What are some of the <u>long</u>-term effects of flooding?
c What is the most <u>cost</u>-effective way to travel in your country?
d How can <u>cross</u>-cultural understanding be best achieved?
e What's the best way of keeping up-to-<u>date</u> with world news?
f What are the advantages and disadvantages of students working part-<u>time</u>?
g Do you like modern buildings or do you prefer them to be more old-<u>fashioned</u>?
h What are the most <u>time</u>-consuming daily activities for you?
i What information can <u>non</u>-verbal communication give us?
j How can you ensure friendships are long-<u>lasting</u>?

6
Student's own answers.

Exam listening

Questions 31–5
31 household tasks
32 generally avoided
33 case studies
34 exact aim
35 multiple choice

Script
I'm sure I'm not alone when I say I'm very good at putting off all those little everyday tasks until the last possible moment. And it seems this procrastination is more widespread than you might think. According to research carried out at Whitehall University last year, almost nine out of ten British people postpone doing certain household tasks until the last possible moment. This figure got me wondering whether it might also be the case that people avoid doing things in their professional or academic lives too. So, today I'm going to talk to you about some research I've been involved in into procrastination, or to put it simply, putting off something that you should be doing now until a later date. This study is linked to the research being undertaken here in the Psychology department on Time Efficiency.

The main purpose of the study was to see how far procrastination affects our everyday lives, both at work and study and at home. It also aimed to identify any common characteristics of serial procrastinators and find out what type of tasks are generally avoided.

So, let's start by looking at how the research was conducted. The first stage involved conducting case studies of 12 people from different walks of life, including full- and part-time students, working and stay-at-home parents, professional and blue-collar workers. The case studies involved asking the subjects to complete a log of tasks and duties performed over a week, including recording details of letters and emails they received during that period. At the end of each day they were asked to record which tasks they had started or completed and which were still to do.

By the way, before the study began, the subjects were told that the research was into workloads and time availability so that at no time during the week's study were any of them aware of the exact aim of the research as it was felt that this might distort the results. At the end of the week the subjects were interviewed in full and the results were analysed.

For the second stage of the research we devised a questionnaire for a cross-section of the population, to find out what type of tasks they avoid doing and for what reasons. The questionnaire contained 16 multiple-choice questions and in total, 80 people were interviewed face-to-face and 20 more completed the questionnaire by email. The results were collated and analysed and these will be discussed a little later.

Questions 36–40

36–38 A, C, E
39, 40 C, E

Script

Moving on to the findings then, and not surprisingly, all 12 subjects showed some degree of task postponement, with over half, that's 7 out of the 12, showing a high degree of procrastination. The results of the survey showed a similar story with an incredible 87% of respondents admitting to some sort of task avoidance at some point, although there were obvious differences in the degree to which respondents delayed tasks.

The two areas of work that were most commonly avoided were at home rather than work or study; DIY jobs head the list, closely followed by domestic admin, er, that's things like household bills and correspondence. Close behind were domestic chores, with ironing and cleaning being the least popular household tasks. Not surprisingly, this task avoidance seemed more prevalent if the undertaking involved a deadline that was still some way off, rather than an urgent one. Typical examples of such tasks were; responding to non-urgent emails, paying bills, and starting assignments, which I'm sure many of you can relate to. As the deadline for a task approached, motivation to complete the task generally increased. What is interesting to note is that the majority of the subjects did not postpone tasks in order to do something more urgent or important. In fact, most appeared to delay starting the jobs in favour of unimportant or non-essential tasks such as having a coffee, a chat on the phone or tidying a desk. Could it be then that the nature of the postponed tasks holds the key

to their delay? Indeed, it seems that the more disagreeable the task seems to the performer, the higher the degree of procrastination involved. More enjoyable and satisfying tasks, like choosing new curtains for the house or replying to emails from friends were generally performed without much delay.

When an analysis of different groups was conducted, it was found that there was no obvious difference between age groups or genders; it seems that you either are a procrastinator or you're not, with age and gender having little relevance. Neither was there a clear link between hours worked or studied and levels of task avoidance. However, there did seem to be one clear distinction and this was between respondents who could be classed as high achievers, erm, that is those with higher-level qualifications and in professional and managerial positions. These people generally seemed to have a lesser degree of procrastination than those with fewer academic qualifications or in more basic or unskilled jobs.

When asked why they avoided tasks, the most widely given answer was lack of time, lack of motivation and particularly where DIY is concerned, lack of skill or confidence to get the job done. The more confident we feel about the task, the less likely we are to procrastinate. But the more we lack confidence in our ability to complete a task, the greater the likelihood is of avoiding it altogether. Respondents to the survey also cited forgetfulness and being easily distracted by other tasks as the reason for avoiding jobs. Another popular reason was not having the self-discipline or will-power, a characteristic often seen in those who find it difficult to lose weight or give up smoking. Indeed, some respondents talked about putting off starting a diet as an example of their procrastination habits.

So, what do these results tell us? The one thing that seems abundantly clear is that, for whatever reason, the vast majority of us have a tendency to procrastinate. Our findings do highlight some general characteristics of procrastinators and the type of tasks avoided.

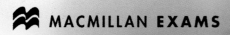

MACMILLAN EXAMS

DIRECT TO

Written by leading IELTS author Sam McCarter, Direct to IELTS provides a short and concise course that combines print and online materials for a more interactive learning experience

- Bands 6.0 – 7.0

- Eight topic-based units cover the skills required for the academic module of the IELTS exam plus grammar and vocabulary build-up

- A 'Writing Bank' provides detailed and focused practice including all task types found in the writing exam and annotated model answers

- The website includes four computer-based practice tests, written by an experienced exam writer, as well as downloadable worksheets to accompany the Student's Book

WITH FOUR **ONLINE** PRACTICE TESTS

IELTS

Student's Book

Sam McCarter

MACMILLAN
EDUCATION

www.directtoielts.com

The IELTS Skills Apps

Exam practice exercises and interactive tasks to help you develop the skills you will need to excel in IELTS.

Courtecy of Apple Inc.

- Written by Sam McCarter, the author of the bestselling *Ready for IELTS* and *Tips for IELTS*
- Each skill is explained and comes with examples and an interactive exercise
- Practise answering the full range of question types that you can expect to find in the IELTS exam

- A detailed overview of the IELTS exam
- Score yourself on the interactive 'Can Do' statement section
- A wide range of innovative and interactive exercises that help you work on the essential skills needed for the IELTS exam

Learn more at the Macmillan Education Apps
website:www.macmillaneducationapps.com